W9-AGM-151

America's Living History

Cuban Missile Crisis

In the Shadow of Nuclear War

R. Conrad Stein

Enslow Publishers, Inc.
40 Industrial Road
Box 398
Berkeley Heights, NJ 07922
USA
http://www.enslow.com

Library of Congress Cataloging-in-Publication Data:

Stein, R. Conrad.
    Cuban Missile Crisis : in the shadow of nuclear war / R. Conrad Stein.
    p. cm.
    Summary: "Discusses the Cuban missile crisis, a thirteen-day struggle between the United States and the Soviet Union, including the causes of the conflict, the leaders faced with important decisions, and the final resolution to avoid nuclear war"—Provided by publisher.
    Includes bibliographical references and index.
    ISBN-13: 978-0-7660-2905-7
    ISBN-10: 0-7660-2905-0
    1. Cuban Missile Crisis, 1962—Juvenile literature. I. Title.
    E841.S734 2009
    972.9106'4—dc22
                                   2008004703

Printed in the United States of America

10 9 8 7 6 5 4 3 2 1

To Our Readers: We have done our best to make sure all Internet Addresses in this book were active and appropriate when we went to press. However, the author and the publisher have no control over and assume no liability for the material available on those Internet sites or on other Web sites they may link to. Any comments or suggestions can be sent by e-mail to comments@enslow.com or to the address on the back cover.

♻ Enslow Publishers, Inc., is committed to printing our books on recycled paper. The paper in every book contains 10% to 30% post-consumer waste (PCW). The cover board on the outside of each book contains 100% PCW. Our goal is to do our part to help young people and the environment too!

Illustration Credits: Associated Press, pp. 10, 16, 21, 38, 40, 59, 63, 70, 74, 80, 84, 98, 100, 102, 106, 111–128; Chris Hammond/Alamy, p. 1; Enslow Publishers, Inc., p. 6; John F. Kennedy Presidential Library and Museum, pp. 8, 50, 56; The Library of Congress, p. 104; National Archives and Records Administration, p. 52; Photographed by Cecil Stoughton, White House, in the John F. Kennedy Presidential Library and Museum, Boston, p. 108; The Granger Collection, New York, pp. 29, 34, 94; Time & Life Pictures/Getty Images, pp. 19, 66, 77, 96; U.S. Air Force, p. 4; U.S. Navy, p. 89.

Cover Illustration: John F. Kennedy Presidential Library and Museum (map); Library of Congress (Kennedy).

Contents

On October 14, 1962, a U-2 spy plane photographed the Soviet military installing missiles in Cuba. The U-2 made its first flight in August 1955.

Chapter 1

On October 14, 1962, the skies were clear and cloudless above the island of Cuba. These were perfect conditions for an operation by America's secret spy plane. At 7:10 in the morning, an American aircraft called a U-2 approached Cuban shores. The U-2 had elongated wings, which allowed it to soar at dizzying heights above the sea and land. It carried sensitive, state-of-the-art cameras. The U-2 was America's eye in the sky. It was a special aircraft, designed to photograph the activities of potential enemies.

Major Richard Heyser, an experienced Air Force pilot, flew the plane. He knew that his flight was dangerous. When the U-2 was first developed in the 1950s, it flew so high that enemy anti-aircraft guns and rockets could not shoot it down. Nor could hostile fighter planes attain the U-2's altitude to fire upon it. But recently developed anti-aircraft rockets were able to hit the U-2 despite its lofty heights. Heyser wore a parachute strapped around his shoulders. However, bailing out in the thin air and freezing temperatures sixty thousand feet above sea level was risky. It was not known if a pilot could survive such a long parachute drop.

In addition, Heyser must have pondered over what would happen to him if he were captured on Cuban soil.

The U-2 operation he flew was a violation of international law. Major Heyser was illegally penetrating the airspace above a sovereign nation. In fact, he could be brought to trial as a spy. Spies are often executed.

This perilous U-2 flight was ordered by President John F. Kennedy. The president had sent several other U-2s over Cuba in recent months. The American president worried about the activities of Russian troops and engineers on the island nation. Agents on the ground told Kennedy that many Russians had recently been

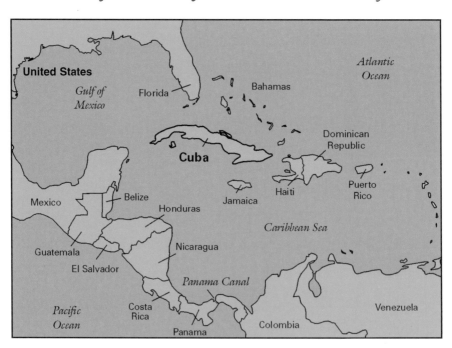

While the United States and the Soviet Union were quite far apart, Cuba was very close to the American state of Florida. If the Soviet Union was able to launch nuclear missiles from Cuba, they could hit the United States and kill millions of people.

stationed on Cuba. Dozens of Russian ships were seen entering and leaving Cuban ports. This was the height of the Cold War, a grim period of tension between the Soviet Union and the United States. Cuba lay just ninety miles from the shores of Florida. What were the Soviets doing there? Kennedy hoped that U-2 photographs would give him and his advisers a clue.

Along the western shores of Cuba, Major Heyser started his cameras. He flew twelve miles above the island and could see no details of the ground. But his cameras were so precise that they took pictures of objects as small as cars and trucks parked on the streets below. The photo run took a little over ten minutes. Heyser then turned and headed home. He landed at McCoy Air Force Base near Orlando, Florida. His mission, though dangerous, proved to be routine. Heyser described it as, "a piece of cake, a milk run."[1]

Film from the U-2 cameras was quickly developed and sent to experts for study. One team of experts was housed above a shabby-looking garage on K Street in Washington, D.C. This was the National

The Soviet Union

Russia's official name was once the Union of Soviet Socialist Republics (the USSR), or the Soviet Union. In terms of area, it was the largest country in the world, stretching from Europe to the Pacific Ocean. The country was formed in 1922 as a union of several republics. The biggest and most important of the republics was Russia. At the time of the Cuban missile crisis, the Soviet Union was commonly—if inaccuratly—referred to as Russia, and its people were called Russians. President Kennedy and other American leaders usually used the word Russians when referring to the Soviet people.

MRBM FIELD LAUNCH SITE
SAN CRISTOBAL NO 1
14 OCTOBER 1962

ERECTOR/LAUNCHER EQUIPMENT

TENT AREAS

EQUIPMENT

ERECTOR/LAUNCHER EQUIPMENT

8 MISSILE TRAILERS

CONSTRUCTION

Military officials showed several images of the missile sites in Cuba to President Kennedy on the morning of October 16. This image was among them.

Photographic Interpretation Center (NPIC), headed by Arthur Lundahl. The NPIC operated out of a garage because the agency wanted to disguise its activities from any possible Russian spies.

At first, the Arthur Lundahl team saw little more than Russian defensive missiles. These were rockets designed to shoot down enemy aircraft. The defensive missiles were recently unpacked from crates and were not yet operational. Still, the new missiles presented a threat. When ready, they could fire upon future U-2 flights. The presence of defensive missiles also meant the Soviets were serious about their intentions in Cuba—whatever those intentions were.

After further study, the NPIC experts discovered a series of shocking photos. In the next few days, they would prove to be pictures that changed the world. Images showed six long narrow objects covered with canvas. To untrained eyes the objects seemed to be no more than large, insignificant boxes. But the canvas-covered articles were the same length and width as Russian medium-range ballistic missiles (MRBMs). The American experts knew the dimensions of MRBMs because those missiles were often paraded through Moscow streets during military celebrations.

The warning signs presented by the U-2 pictures stunned the photo-analyzing group. A Russian MRBM was designed to carry an atomic bomb. It had sufficient range to reach Washington, D.C., or New York City when launched from Cuba. Each MRBM with a nuclear-tipped warhead was capable of destroying an American city and killing millions of people.

Arthur Lundahl called his boss, Ray Cline, deputy director of the U.S. Central Intelligence Agency (CIA). Monitoring the enemy was the CIA's primary mission.

Lundahl knew he had important, even earthshaking news for the CIA. Over the phone, he thought about the turmoil this would cause, "when you tell him [about the missiles]."[2]

"Him," was President John F. Kennedy.

The man chosen to inform Kennedy of the discovery

Major Richard "Steve" Heyser, left, and General Curtis LeMay, center, meet with President John F. Kennedy at the White House in 1962. They are there to discuss Heyser's U-2 spy plane photos of Soviet ballistic missile sites.

was McGeorge Bundy, a special assistant to the president. Bundy waited until Monday morning October 16 to tell Kennedy the distressing news. He could have wakened Kennedy during the night, but chose not to do so.

Early in the morning of October 16, Bundy found the president still in his pajamas and reading a newspaper. He told him of the U-2 pictures. The president said, "He can't do this to me."[3]

"He" was the Soviet premier, Nikita Khrushchev.

October 16, 1962, marked the beginning of the Cuban missile crisis. In the days to come, the world held its breath as Kennedy and Khrushchev dueled with words, threats, manipulations, and negotiations. Thousands of troops on all sides stood poised for war. Most frightening of all, hundreds of nuclear bombs and missile warheads were armed and made ready. No one knew exactly what would happen if such a vast arsenal of atomic bombs were fired. Many scientists believed a nuclear exchange between Russia and the United States would end life on Earth.

With fear in their hearts, people of all nations watched the October 1962 struggle between two nuclear superpowers. It was an unforgettable episode in history that lasted for thirteen tension-filled days. Never before or since have we come so close to the end of the world.

Chapter 2

[F]rom Stettin in the Baltic to Trieste in the Adriatic, an Iron Curtain has descended across the [European] Continent.[1]

> —The British leader Winston Churchill, speaking at Fulton, Missouri, on March 5, 1946

Many historians regard Churchill's famous Fulton, Missouri, speech as the official beginning of the Cold War.

One War Ends; Another Begins

Early in the morning of April 25, 1945, a platoon of about thirty-five American soldiers patrolled near the Elbe River south of Berlin, Germany. The men walked with caution. All had survived many months of bitter warfare. Now the war in Europe was coming to a close. In the countryside, German soldiers were surrendering in large numbers. For five years, Europe had been held in the grip of World War II. Finally, it seemed, the conflict was near the end.

The American officer leading the platoon spotted troops on the east side of the Elbe. He knew the Russian army was close by. The officer peered at the soldiers across the river through his binoculars. They did not appear to be German. From their uniforms, he determined the men on the far side of the Elbe were Russian infantrymen.

Russians! This meant the fighting, at least in this one sector, was over. The Soviet Union and the United States were allies in the war against Nazi Germany. For many months, the American army had marched toward Germany from the west while Russian forces approached the enemy nation from the east. Now soldiers of the two sides were about to meet on German soil. The Russians and the Americans shouted and waved at one another. The relief every soldier felt was overwhelming. On this patch of ground, peace prevailed after many horrible years of war.

Germany surrendered twelve days after the historic meeting on the Elbe. On September 2, 1945, Japan, an ally of Germany, signed surrender documents, but only after the United States had dropped atomic bombs on two Japanese cities. World War II ended. The war, which began in Europe in 1939, was the bloodiest conflict in human history. More than fifty million people died as a result of the fighting. Most of the deaths were civilians.

Sadly, the end of World War II saw the beginning of a new conflict called the Cold War. It was not a war of battles and mass deaths. Instead, it was a long period of high tension as two rival countries—the Soviet Union and the United States—fought what was often a war of words. Both states had large military forces and powerful economies. In the years after World War II, no country on Earth could challenge the two giants. Journalists referred to the Soviet Union and the United States as the world's superpowers.

The USSR and the United States were guided by opposing economic philosophies. The Soviets believed in a Communist form of government. The word *Communism* comes from Latin and means "belonging to all." Under Communism, the government owns all large stores, factories, farms, and other businesses. The means of distributing food and other goods are in government hands also. The Americans operated under a free-enterprise system. That system allows individuals to own businesses and keep the profits (capital) earned by them. The free-enterprise structure is called capitalism.

The USSR was the world's leading Communist nation. The Soviets imposed Communism to Eastern European countries such as Poland and Czechoslovakia. Those countries had little choice but to accept Communism because the system of government was forced upon them by the Soviet army. The USSR and the European Communist nations were called Iron Curtain countries after the famous 1946 Winston Churchill speech. In 1949, a revolution succeeded in China and that nation emerged with a Communist government. After 1949, China and Russia were rivals and competed with each other to lead the Communist world. But Americans tended to believe all Communist nations were united in their desire to impose their form of government on others.

During the Cold War, anti-Communism rose to an almost religious zeal in the United States. Politicians gained favor with voters by accusing rivals as being "soft on Communism." One of the most famous anti-Communist crusaders was Joseph McCarthy, a senator from Wisconsin. In the early 1950s, McCarthy claimed he had discovered Communist spies holding key positions in the U.S. government. The senator said that Communists and those who favored Communism operated in the State Department and even in the army. Critics claimed McCarthy was simply seeking fame and called his anti-Communist campaign a "witch hunt."

In June 1950, Communist North Korea invaded capitalistic South Korea. The United States sent troops to bolster South Korean forces. Months after the initial invasion, China moved a large army into North Korea and fought the American-led forces. The Korean War lasted from 1950 until a cease-fire was put in place in 1953. The conflict was a "hot" chapter in the Cold War. As is true with most wars, Korea was a tragedy. The Americans suffered 33,629 battle deaths.[2] The true figure of Koreans killed in the war is not known.

Somewhere in Korea, on August 28, 1950, an American infantryman, his buddy killed in action in the Korean War, weeps on the shoulder of another soldier. Meanwhile, a corpsman, left, goes about the business of filling out casualty tags.

Many Americans believed the Korean War was orchestrated from Moscow, the Russian capital. Americans saw little difference between a Russian Communist, a Chinese Communist, or a North Korean Communist. However, the Communist countries had different goals based on their own national interests. But according to American thinking, all Communists sought world dominance. The Russian people held similar negative feelings about capitalism and the United States.

Freezes and Thaws

In 1948, the city of West Berlin in Germany was an island of capitalism perched in a Communist-ruled land. According to the terms of a complicated post-World War II agreement, Germany was divided into eastern and western halves. The Soviet Union occupied East Germany while the United States and its allies reigned in West Germany. Berlin, too, was divided into eastern and western districts. Both East Berlin and West Berlin lay deep in East German territory. Therefore Berlin loomed as a battleground in the Cold War.

On June 24, 1948, the Soviet Union closed all roads and train lines leading to West Berlin. The Soviets did not explain the sudden move. Clearly the road closures were Cold War manipulations. West Berlin held 2.5 million people. Cut off from supplies, the West Berliners would have to give up their status as a capitalistic city and join the Communist fold. President Harry S. Truman defied the Soviets by ordering the Berlin Airlift. For the next eleven months, U.S. Air Force planes flew supplies to West Berlin. Planes carried food, medicine, and even coal to heat apartments. Finally, on May 12, 1949, the Soviet Union ended its blockade.

The Berlin Airlift was a freeze—a major crisis—in the Cold War. Never did Soviet and American armies directly fight each other during the Cold War. Instead, the Cold War was characterized by heightened fear and tension during incidents such as the 1948 Berlin blockade. Times of high tension were called "freezes" in the Cold War. Periods of relaxation, called "thaws," often set in after a crisis was resolved.

On May 1, 1960, a major Cold War freeze was triggered by the flight of an American U-2 spy plane. President Dwight D. Eisenhower ordered a series of U-2 flights over Soviet territory. The president wanted to learn more about Russian progress in building long-range missiles. The flights were authorized despite the existence of a thaw in Cold War tensions. The U-2 aircraft was shot down by a newly developed Russian missile. The pilot, Francis Gary Powers, managed to parachute out of his crippled aircraft and was captured. Soviet premier Nikita Khrushchev demanded an apology for this act of espionage. President Eisenhower admitted the U-2 was on a spying mission, but he refused to apologize. A Soviet court convicted Francis Gary Powers of espionage and he spent twenty-one months in Russian prisons before being released.

Tensions over the U-2 incident remained high when Premier Khrushchev met newly elected President Kennedy

U.S. and Soviet tanks face off over the Berlin wall, which was built by Russians to split the city and deny access to the Soviet-controlled Eastern sector of the city.

When the Berlin Wall Fell

For almost thirty years, the Berlin Wall remained, dividing the two cities. It stood as a grim reminder of the Cold War. On the night of November 11, 1989, Berliners gathered on both sides of the infamous Berlin Wall. Amid cheers and singing, they began tearing the wall down. Communism was no longer the threat it once was. Many Eastern European states had already adopted capitalistic economies. The Soviet Union had weakened. By 1991, the once mighty union had broken up into different republics. Historians regard the tearing down of the Berlin Wall as the symbolic end of the Cold War.

in Vienna, Austria, in June of 1961. Khrushchev demanded a final resolution of the Berlin situation. Kennedy refused to change the status in Berlin. At the time, many hundreds of East Berliners were fleeing Communism to become residents of West Berlin. To put a stop to these escapes, the Soviets built a long barbed-wire-clad wall between the two Berlins. Berliners called it a Schandmauer, meaning a "wall of shame."

The Arms Race

Adding to the tensions of the Cold War was the deadly contest between the two superpowers to build destructive weapons. The United States was first to develop and use the atomic bomb, or A-bomb. An atomic bomb was dropped on the Japanese city of Hiroshima on August 6, 1945, and another on the city of Nagasaki three days later. The A-bomb that fell on Hiroshima killed more than seventy thousand people in a matter of minutes. The two bombs prompted Japanese leaders to surrender and finally end the war.

On August 9, 1945, an American bomber dropped an atomic bomb on Nagasaki, Japan. The bomb killed tens of thousands of civilians and created a mushroom cloud high in the atmosphere.

In August 1949, the Soviet Union tested its first atomic bomb. Both Cold War rival nations labored to build more and better A-bombs. The new bombs they created made the Hiroshima bomb look primitive by comparison. In 1952, American scientists exploded a hydrogen bomb (H-bomb), which was many times more powerful than an atomic bomb. One year later, the Soviets developed their own H-bomb.

By devising more and more destructive bombs, the two sides achieved what newspaper writers called a balance of power. This balance meant that the Russians and the Americans possessed arsenals powerful enough to destroy each other many times over. Some writers and historians believed that the existence of the bombs actually prevented nuclear war, as one side was afraid of attacking the other for fear of being annihilated by a return strike. A-bombs were weapons of indescribable terror. So, the standoff between the two nations was also called the balance of terror. Military generals had their own term for the vast arsenal of nuclear arms possessed by the two sides. The generals referred to the weapons balance as mutually assured destruction, often stated by its initials: MAD. The word *mad*, of course, also means illogical, insane, and senseless.

Russian atomic weapons stirred up grave fears in the United States. Cities built nuclear bomb shelters where citizens could take refuge in case of an attack. Chicago's downtown bomb shelter doubled as an underground parking lot, which serves the city today. Thousands of homeowners built family bomb shelters in their backyards. Plans for digging do-it-yourself shelters appeared in magazines such as *Popular Mechanics* and in newspapers.

Government-issued movies and pamphlets advised Americans on how to protect themselves if caught in the open during an A-bomb attack. The first thing one would see in such an attack would be a bright flash in the sky. Upon seeing the flash, citizens were told to "duck and cover." This meant a person was to crouch down and cover up all exposed skin in order to shield oneself from the searing heat of the blast. Civilian defense agencies made a special cartoon, which appeared on television. On TV screens, a turtle danced into sight singing a happy tune that included the words "duck and cover." Then came a bright flash, and the turtle disappeared into his shell. Schools conducted A-bomb drills on a regular basis. At a command by the teacher, all students quickly ducked under their desks.

But would the drills and the shelters allow people to survive a nuclear attack? Many experts predicted the true results of a massive A-bomb raid would be catastrophic beyond anyone's imagination. Blasts from atomic bombs release dangerous radiation that poisons the air and the soil. Radiation causes sickness and death long after the initial explosion. Even those men and women who survived the first blasts would be exposed to deadly radiation. In an all-out war between Russia and the United States, hundreds and even thousands of bombs would detonate over the two countries. Radiation produced by such nuclear exchange could destroy all life on the earth.

The Doomsday Movies

Books and movies of the Cold War era treated the possibility of a doomsday caused by nuclear war. Two popular movies, seen by millions of Americans, were *On the Beach* (1959) and *Doctor Strangelove* (1964).

On the Beach opens after a nuclear war. Radiation has killed everyone on the earth except the people in Australia. The Australians know that radiation clouds will soon drift over their land and kill them, too. An American submarine flees to Australia. The submarine commander and an Australian woman fall in love despite the approach of deadly radiation.

Amazingly, *Doctor Strangelove* is a comedy about a nuclear doomsday. The movie features a bumbling American president, a drunken Soviet premier, and a madman American general who sends his bombers flying off to drop atomic bombs on the Soviet Union. The film's full name was *Dr. Strangelove or: How I Learned to Stop Worrying and Love the Bomb.*

Both movies, though dated, are interesting to watch today as they present a time when the world was in the grips of Cold War fears and tensions.

It was not known for certain if nuclear war would usher in doomsday and snuff out life on the planet. But the doomsday possibility was real and the concept staggered the thinking of rational people. For billions of years, planet Earth had spawned life. Now, with one massive nuclear exchange between the two superpowers, Earth could be reduced to a dusty, lifeless ball speeding around the Sun.

During the arms race, the two superpowers labored under a "never again" policy. Both the United States and the USSR were woefully unprepared for World War II. When war broke out, they had poorly equipped and poorly trained armed forces. Consequently, the two countries suffered terrible early defeats. Now they vowed never again to be caught unready for armed conflict. The Soviets and the Americans poured money into their defense establishments. Their scientists worked to develop more efficient airplanes, rockets, and bombs.

The A-bombs that fell on Japan were delivered by aircraft, huge B-29 bombers. During World War II, the piston engine B-29 was the pride of the American bomber fleet. In the Cold War, piston-powered aircraft were replaced by jet bombers such as the huge B-52. However, jet aircraft, too, could be shot down, and scientists looked to missiles to deliver nuclear weapons.

The ultimate delivery system was the ballistic missile. Such missiles were launched into the sky and plunged downward at thousands of miles an hour. In the 1950s and early 1960s, no weapons existed that could destroy a ballistic missile in flight. Soviet and American scientists labored to develop huge long-range missiles, which were seen as the ultimate and the unstoppable weapons of the Cold War.

Space exploration was a positive byproduct of the missile contest. The same rockets designed to shoot nuclear warheads at enemy nations could also be used to propel objects into space. On October 4, 1957, the Soviet Union shocked the world by launching *Sputnik I* into the heavens. *Sputnik* (a Russian word for traveler) was the first human-made earth-orbiting vehicle. The satellite launch was a great scientific breakthrough, but even space was viewed as a competitive field in the rivalry between Russia and America. In Cold War terms, the Soviet Union had gained first place in what came to be called the space race. Less than two years after *Sputnik*, another Soviet spacecraft, *Luna I*, zoomed past the moon. Early Russian successes in the space race were bitter blows to American prestige. Finally, American scientists and engineers won the space race by sending men to the moon in July 1969.

But before the American success, another political issue hotly debated in the United States was the status of Cuba. In October 1962, the island nation, so near to U.S. shores, became a focal point in the most dangerous clash ever between the two nuclear superpowers.

Chapter 3

Thus the dominant feeling was one of shocked incredulity. We had been deceived by Khrushchev, but we had also fooled ourselves. No official within the government had ever suggested to President Kennedy that the Russian buildup in Cuba would include missiles.[1]

> —Robert F. Kennedy, from his book *Thirteen Days: A Memoir of the Cuban Missile Crisis.*

On his famous first voyage in 1492, Christopher Columbus landed on the island of Cuba. Columbus was an Italian sea captain sailing for Spain. Other Spaniards soon followed Columbus and built outposts on Cuba and on islands in the Caribbean Sea.

Spanish Cuba

The Spaniards were invaders. The native people of Cuba resisted the occupation of their island. But the natives had little chance in their battles against the Spaniards. Spanish soldiers carried guns and they were mounted on horses. No one in the New World—the Caribbean and the Americas—had ever seen a firearm or a horse before.

The island of Cuba emerged as a naval hub for the great empire the Spaniards established in the Americas. That empire included present-day Mexico and extended into Central America and South America. For three hundred years, the Spanish flag waved over its vast holdings. Then, in the 1820s, independence movements broke out in

27

Mexico and South America. In less than a decade, Spain lost practically all of its possessions in the Western Hemisphere. Only Cuba and the island of Puerto Rico remained in the Spanish fold.

Independence movements began in Cuba also. The movements failed, but they instilled a spirit of liberty within the Cuban people. Cubans longed for the day when they would rise as a nation free of all foreign rule.

Cuba and the United States

Early in its history, the United States sought to keep European powers from building colonies in the Western Hemisphere. Americans feared that such colonies could serve as military bases and threaten the United States. In 1823, President James Monroe gave a famous speech to Congress, in which he announced the Monroe Doctrine. The Monroe Doctrine warned European nations to not establish military bases or other enclaves in the Americas.

Some American politicians viewed the Spanish presence in Cuba as a violation of the Monroe Doctrine. In the late 1800s, the United States favored Cuban independence. By 1895, a war for independence raged on the island. President William McKinley sent the battleship *Maine* to the port of Havana in 1898. The president hoped the giant battleship with Marines on board would

During the Spanish-American War, naval battles were fought near the Philippines, Puerto Rico, and Cuba. The Battle of Manila Bay (above) was fought near the Philippines on May 1, 1898.

protect the many American citizens who lived and ran businesses in Cuba.

February 15, 1898, dawned a calm and peaceful day in Havana. Suddenly, a terrible explosion shook the port city. The battleship *Maine* blew up and quickly sank in the waters of Havana Harbor. In the disaster, 266 American naval men lost their lives.[2] The cause of the explosion remains a mystery. Today, historians believe that a fire, started by accident within the ship, triggered the terrible blast. But many Americans, especially members of the press, claimed Spanish naval forces had blown up the *Maine* with an underwater mine. Newspapers called for war. In April 1898, the U.S. Congress declared war on Spain. The battle cry rang out: "Remember the *Maine!*"

The Spanish-American War was short, and it was a decisive victory for the United States. A treaty signed on December 12, 1898, gave the United States control over Puerto Rico and Cuba as well as the Philippines in the Pacific Ocean.

To Cuban revolutionaries, the result of the war was deeply disappointing. In their view, Cuba had gone from being a Spanish possession to being a colony of the powerful United States. Cuba was proclaimed an independent country in 1902. But the United States forced the new Cuban government to accept the Platt Amendment to its constitution. This amendment was an extension of the Monroe Doctrine. It said the United States was entitled to intervene and send forces to the island if future revolutionary warfare broke out. Also, the United States was given a permanent naval base on Cuban soil at Guantánamo Bay. The United States operates the Guantánamo naval base to this day.

Cuban nationals called the Platt Amendment and the naval base examples of "Yankee imperialism." This form of imperialism occurs when Americans, sometimes called Yankees, bully their weaker Latin American neighbors. The charge of Yankee imperialism spread to Cuba's economy. American business interests bought land in newly independent Cuba and operated companies there. By the 1920s, foreign companies, mainly American, controlled 80 percent of the Cuban sugar industry.[3] Investors from the United States bought into the Cuban railroad system and owned electrical power companies. Tourism thrived as Americans and Europeans flocked to Cuba's marvelous beaches. Many of the best hotels and restaurants that served the tourists were owned by U.S. companies. American gangsters bought night clubs in Havana and operated gambling casinos in the city.

The contrast between the lives of wealthy Americans and Cuban workers was glaring. Fruit pickers for the Boston-based United Fruit Company earned less than a dollar a day.[4] The pickers lived in tiny shacks on the outskirts of the company's vast fields. American employees of United Fruit resided in gated communities with swimming

Guantánamo and Controversy

After the terrorist attacks on September 11, 2001, the U.S. naval base at Guantánamo Bay in Cuba was used as a prison camp to house suspected terrorists. American laws that protect individuals accused of crimes do not apply on the Cuban base. Critics claim that the accused held at Guantánamo are denied the right to a fair trial. Some insist that the United States practices forms of torture at Guantánamo.

pools and golf courses. Cuban hotel employees, too, were underpaid. They watched with bitterness as foreign tourists spent more on a single meal than they earned in a week.

In 1933, an army sergeant named Fulgencio Batista rose to power in Cuba. For most of the next twenty-five years, Batista controlled the country either as its president or as the power behind the presidency. Batista was a dictator, but American leaders favored him. Communism was on the rise in Cuba. Batista declared himself to be anti-Communism.

Cubans felt betrayed by their government and overwhelmed by the influence of American dollars. They sought a hero who could lead them out of their despair.

Fidel Castro

Fidel Castro was born August 13, 1926, near the town of Mayari, Cuba. His father was a Spanish immigrant who owned a fruit plantation. In contrast to most Cubans, Fidel grew up in comfortable middle-class circumstances. As a young man, he attended law school. But revolutionary politics was his greatest passion. In 1953, he tried to overthrow the Batista government by leading an attack on the Moncada army barracks. The effort failed and Castro was sent to jail.

After serving two years in prison, Castro and his younger brother Raúl traveled to Mexico. The Castro brothers formed the 26th of July Movement, so named after the assault on the Moncada barracks. In December 1956, Castro and his group boarded a small boat and sailed for Cuba. The boat was built to hold about a dozen men, but eighty-two Castro followers squeezed aboard.[5] The vessel leaked badly. Only by a minor miracle did it manage to reach Cuban shores.

Once on land, the men of the 26th of July Movement fought Batista's soldiers. Most of the revolutionaries were killed or captured. The Castro brothers and about a dozen others fled to the mountains to carry on the revolution. During this mountain exile, Castro rose in the eyes of Cubans. He became an exciting and dashing figure. He launched hit-and-run raids on Batista's forces. He broadcast revolutionary messages through a secret radio station.

On New Year's Day 1959, the 26th of July Movement triumphed. Castro and his men occupied Havana. Batista fled the country. At first, the American public cheered Castro's victory. Batista was known for corruption and cruelty. Many Americans compared Castro to Robin Hood, the folk hero of old England, who fought against a greedy king.

But while the American people admired Castro, the U.S. government and American business interests were wary of the man. In those Cold War days, the question loomed: Was Castro a Communist? Raúl Castro openly

Fidel Castro (right) and Ernesto "Che" Guevara, another revolutionary, speak at their encampment in the Sierra Maestra mountains of Cuba in the 1950s.

proclaimed Communist sympathies. Fidel Castro, at first, was more of a mystery. On a 1959 trip to the United States he declared, "We are against all kinds of dictators. . . . That is why we are against communism."[6]

Once he was in complete control over Cuba, Fidel Castro passed laws that broke up large plantations. Some of those plantations were owned by Americans. Castro redistributed the plantation land to small Cuban farmers. Castro soon acted as a dictator himself. Shortly after his rise to power, Fidel Castro ordered the execution of 521 Batista's former followers.[7]

By 1960, Castro had lost much of his popularity with the American people. His crackdown on political opponents within Cuba made him appear almost a bad as Batista had been. Also, Castro was too cozy with the Soviets. Key members of his government had traveled to the Soviet Union and conferred with Communist leaders.

Secretly the U.S. government launched plans to dispose of Fidel Castro. Some of the schemes hatched by American leaders were bizarre. An attempt was made to lace one of Fidel's favorite cigars with a mind-altering drug that would make him sound incoherent during a radio address to the nation.[8] American authorities even contacted Florida gangsters, who knew Cuba well, to hire hit men and assassinate the Cuban leader.[9]

The American people were entirely unaware of these moves against Castro. The 1950s and early 1960s were innocent years. Americans would be shocked to know their government actually planned to kill the leader of another country. Most Americans of the time believed that only Communist countries or dictatorships practiced assassination.

On April 17, 1961, an army of fourteen hundred Cuban exiles landed on the Bay of Pigs in southern Cuba.[10] These men were anti-Castro Cubans who had fled the island when he took power. They now returned in force to rally the people against Castro. At first, American leaders claimed they had nothing to do with this invasion. In truth, the operation was backed by the CIA. Its operatives recruited the men and trained them in hidden Central American bases.

The Bay of Pigs invasion was an utter failure. It had been planned under President Eisenhower. President Kennedy inherited the operation when he took office early in 1961. The Kennedy team wanted to disguise American involvement in the attack and canceled much of the planned air support. Most members of the exile army were forced to surrender. Embarrassed, President Kennedy finally admitted his government's role in the botched invasion. Kennedy said, "There's an old saying that victory has a hundred fathers and defeat is an orphan."[11]

To those Cuban people loyal to Castro, the failed Bay of Pigs operation was another vile example of Yankee imperialism. Now, at last, they had a leader strong enough to fight back against what they saw as the American bullies. After the Bay of Pigs, Fidel Castro was hailed as the savior of Cuba.

Despite the Bay of Pigs disaster, John F. Kennedy was still determined to topple Fidel Castro. He launched Operation Mongoose, a series of covert actions designed to overthrow or even kill the Cuban leader.[12]

In December 1961, Castro declared he was a Communist and that he was building a Communist state in Cuba. Then, in July 1962, Raúl Castro visited the Soviet Union. During that visit, Nikita Khrushchev told the Castro brother that the United States had plans—however incomplete at this point—to invade Cuba. Khrushchev offered to put Soviet missiles on Cuban soil. The Soviet leader made the point that the presence of such missiles would deter the United States from any further invasions. The Castro government accepted the offer. This missile agreement was, of course, made in strict secrecy between Cuba and the Soviet Union. Neither government wanted the United States to know that missiles were about to be placed on an island less than one hundred miles from American soil.

Cuban leader Fidel Castro, left, is hugged by Soviet Premier Nikita Khrushchev on the floor of the United Nations General Assembly in September 1960.

Chapter 4

Every idiot can start a war, but it is impossible to win this war. Therefore the missiles have one purpose—to scare them.[1]

> —Nikita Khrushchev, speaking in a private conversation shortly after he ordered the deployment of missiles to Cuba.

Day One: Tuesday, October 16, 1962

At 9:00 A.M., Robert Kennedy received an urgent call from his brother, President John F. Kennedy. Robert Kennedy was the nation's attorney general. He was also one of the president's most trusted advisers. Years later, Robert wrote:

> *President Kennedy . . . asked me to come to the White House. He said only that we were facing great trouble. . . . That was the beginning of the Cuban missile crisis—a confrontation between the two giant atomic nations, the U.S. and the U.S.S.R., which brought the world to the abyss of nuclear destruction and the end of mankind.*[2]

At 11:45 A.M., an emergency meeting began in the White House. Present at the meeting were President Kennedy, Attorney General Robert Kennedy, Vice President Lyndon Johnson, Secretary of State Dean Rusk, Secretary of Defense Robert McNamara, Army general Maxwell Taylor, United Nations ambassador Adlai Stevenson,

President John F. Kennedy (right) asked his brother Attorney General Robert Kennedy (center) to come to the White House for a meeting on the Cuban missile sites. This photo is from an earlier meeting the two had at the White House on February 28, 1962. Vice President Lyndon Johnson is at the left.

and other high-ranking Kennedy advisers. These men made up the Kennedy team. The next thirteen days would see them working in a frenzy. The men got little sleep and ate meals only in a rush.

Photo experts showed the Kennedy team pictures taken by the U-2 flight. The pictures revealed workers on the ground clearing a field. At first glance, the clearing looked insignificant, almost like a football field. But the experts insisted it would be used to construct a missile-launching site. Small rectangular shapes seen near the field were the actual rocket launchers. The people who interpreted the photos concluded that the missiles would be ready for firing in about ten days. Robert Kennedy later wrote: "The dominant feeling at the meeting was stunned surprise. No one had expected or anticipated that the Russians would deploy surface-to-surface ballistic missiles in Cuba."[3]

The weapons being installed were medium range ballistic missiles (MRBMs), with a range of about 600 to 1,900 miles, and intermediate range ballistic missiles (IRBMs), with a range of about 1,900 to 3,100 miles. Both missile types were born as part of the great arms race between the superpowers. Much larger intercontinental ballistic missiles (ICBMs) had ranges of more than 3,100 miles. Naturally, it was easier to build an IRBM than it was an ICBM. During the presidential campaign of 1960, then candidate Kennedy complained the nation had fallen into a "missile gap" in its competition with the Russians. But this so-called gap simply did not exist. In late 1962, the United States had far more ICBMs than the Soviets.[4] Kennedy and his team believed the Soviet deployment was Khrushchev's way of equalizing the nuclear balance of power. Missiles in Cuba meant a quick and cheap advance for the Russians in their deadly arms race with the United States.

There was little debate on the part of the Kennedy team that the missiles, when ready, would be armed with nuclear warheads. Clearly the Russians would not deploy these rockets to carry anything but their most powerful bombs. Therefore, each missile the Soviets installed was fully capable of eradicating an American city. Given the range of the rockets, the entire eastern half of the United States—including the cities of New York and Washington, D.C.—could be hit by nuclear weapons launched from Cuba.

The United States, too, employed the strategy of putting IRBMs in allied countries near the enemy. At the time of the crisis, American IRBMs were in Great Britain, Italy, and Turkey, ready to be fired. Every one of those IRBMs carried nuclear warheads and was aimed at a target somewhere in the Soviet Union. The missiles in Turkey were particularly upsetting to the Russians. Turkey shared a common border with the Soviet Union. The missiles in Turkey stood almost literally in the Soviet Union's backyard.

The members of the Kennedy team were determined to do something to remove the Cuban missiles. Robert Kennedy said of the team, "They were men of the highest intelligence, industrious, courageous, and dedicated to their country's well-being."[5]

At some time shortly after the meeting started, President Kennedy reached under his conference table and silently pressed a button. The button activated a hidden tape recorder. Kennedy was a writer and a historian and wanted to someday write a history of his presidency. Therefore he taped all important conferences. No one at the conference table, except perhaps for Robert Kennedy, knew their words were being recorded.[6]

Recordings of deliberations during the missile crisis were released in 1997 in a book called *The Kennedy Tapes*. The tapes replay the arguments and counterarguments that determined peace or war. However, the tapes are an incomplete record. During many group discussions, President Kennedy simply did not turn the machine on. Also, some of the tapes are of poor quality, despite the fact that the president's recording device was the best available at the time.

The team considered an air strike to "take out" the missiles with conventional bombs. According to the Kennedy tapes, the debate went as follows:

> **President Kennedy:** *How effective can the take-out be, do they think?*
> **General Maxwell Taylor:** *It'll never be a 100 percent, Mr. President, we know. We hope to take out the vast majority [of missiles] in the first strike, but this is not just one thing—one strike . . . but continuous air attack for whenever necessary . . . .*
> **President Kennedy:** *Well, let's say we just take out the missile bases. Then they have some more there. Obviously they can get them in by submarine and so on.*[7]

All team members gave their opinions. Should the navy blockade Cuba? Should the Marines invade the island? Soviet soldiers and technicians would no doubt be killed in any military action. How would Khrushchev react to the death of his own men?

At the conclusion of the first-day's meeting, Kennedy ordered more U-2 flights. He also required absolute secrecy about the Cuban situation. At this point, the general public had no idea that the Soviets were building missile bases a mere ninety miles away from Florida. Nor did the Russians know that the president and his staff were aware of their missile program. October 16, 1962, came and went, seemingly like a normal day.

Day Two: Wednesday, October 17, 1962

In the morning, President Kennedy traveled to Connecticut to make a campaign speech for a fellow Democrat running for Congress. The speech had been on his schedule for months. The president wanted to abide by his schedule as if nothing unusual was afoot. To break his schedule would alert the country and the press that something urgent was happening in the world.

In Washington, the Kennedy team continued its high-stakes meetings. The team was now called ExComm, which stood for Executive Committee of the U.S. National Security Council.

ExComm met in a seventh-floor office of the State Department building in Washington. The men examined new U-2 photos and found them frightening. Missiles were now visible. The fields being cleared for launch sites swarmed with Russian and Cuban workers. Work was going at a faster pace than the ExComm members originally thought. It appeared as if some of the missiles would be operational in a week or less. Robert Kennedy did the grim arithmetic and wrote: ". . . the estimate was that within a few minutes of [the missiles] being fired 80 million Americans would be dead."[8]

What were Khrushchev's motives for threatening the United States in this manner? Never before had the Russians stationed nuclear weapons beyond their borders. Not even the Iron Curtain countries of Eastern Europe held atomic devices. Also, in recent conferences with U.S. officials, the Soviets claimed they were putting no offensive missiles in Cuba. The distinction between offensive and defensive weapons was critical. It was known that the Russians were installing anti-aircraft rockets in Cuba. But those rockets were designed to shoot down attacking aircraft and thus were considered defensive in nature. All countries had a right to defend their soil. However there was nothing defensive about Soviet IRBMs with warheads aimed at the United States.

Khrushchev's memoirs were published in 1970 as a book called *Khrushchev Remembers*. In the book, he claimed he put missiles in Cuba only to protect that country from another American invasion. In this manner, he was acting as a proper Communist, working to spread Communism to other lands. Khrushchev wrote: "If Cuba fell [to the capitalistic United States], other Latin American countries would reject us, claiming that for all our might the Soviet Union hadn't been able to do any-thing for Cuba except to make empty protests."[9]

By this time, Fidel Castro was an admitted Communist and it was assumed that he, too, accepted the mission of expanding the Communist system. He hoped to encourage other Latin American governments to accept Communism. But Castro had a more immediate goal. He wanted to prevent another American attack on his island nation. To assist him in this goal, he turned to the leader of the powerful Soviet Union.

Nikita Khrushchev was born in 1894 in the Russian village of Kalinkova. His family was impoverished. Neither of his parents knew how to read or write. Khrushchev was attracted to Communism as a young man because he believed the system gave working-class people a better life. He joined the Communist Party and rose to a position second only to Joseph Stalin, the Soviet premier. Stalin was a ruthless dictator who jailed and murdered his opponents. When Stalin died in 1953, Khrushchev even-tually took charge of the USSR. Once in power, he denounced Stalin for his cruel and dictatorial rule.

Promising greater prosperity for the Soviet people, Khrushchev launched new farming and building projects. As a diplomat, he traveled the world preaching the glories of Communism. He portrayed himself as a factory worker with little refinement. Stocky and muscular looking, he used body language to express his moods. He shook with laughter when amused. When angry, he trembled, grew red faced, and shouted at opponents. During a meeting at the United Nations, he once took off his shoe and banged it on a desk to demand attention.

Members of ExComm knew Khrushchev's background and his personality. They also recognized him as a shrewd opponent. By putting missiles in Cuba, he most certainly had other issues in mind rather than simply the expansion of Communism. Perhaps he was pressuring the United States in Cuba in order to win concessions in Berlin. American missiles in Turkey were an embarrassment as well as a threat to the Soviets. Perhaps he thought the missiles on America's doorstep would give his rivals a taste of their own poison.

Whatever Khrushchev's motives were, all ExComm men agreed the Cuban missiles must go. The team pondered two main actions: an air strike and a naval blockade. Both were acts of war. Both proposed actions contained grave dangers for the world. Secretary of Defense Robert McNamara urged a blockade. Aerial bombing would kill many Cubans and Russians. Such an attack would perhaps give Khrushchev no alternative but to strike back. A blockade meant surrounding Cuba with U.S. naval ships. The American ships would intercept incoming vessels, and thus prevent new missiles and crews from reaching the island. The blockade would do nothing about the missiles already in place. But, McNamara hoped the blockade would not cost lives—at least not at the beginning.

Day Three: Thursday, October 18, 1962

ExComm men were beginning to divide into "hawks" and "doves," although none of the team members used those terms. The hawks favored aggressive action against the missiles. Doves urged less drastic means. The doves suggested conferring with Khrushchev and trying to get him to remove the missiles peacefully.

The leading hawk was Air Force general Curtis LeMay. During World War II, LeMay was an aggressive general who led bomber forces. He was the primary planner of massive fire-bombing raids, which the United States launched on Japanese cities. The raids reduced the cities to ashes and killed thousands of people. A stern, unsmiling man, LeMay now urged an immediate all-out air strike on the Cuban missiles.

President Kennedy listened to LeMay's arguments for an air raid on Cuba. He asked how the Russians were likely to respond to such an attack from the sky.

"They'll do nothing," said LeMay.

"Are you trying to tell me that they'll let us bomb their missiles, and kill a lot of Russians and then do nothing?" Kennedy said. "If they don't do anything in Cuba, then they'll certainly do something in Berlin."[10]

Later, back in his office, Kennedy exclaimed, "Can you imagine LeMay saying a thing like that? If we listen to them [the hawkish generals], and do what they want us to do, none of us will be alive later to tell them that they were wrong."[11]

The most influential dove was Adlai Stevenson, America's ambassador to the United Nations. Stevenson was respected around the world for his intellectual approach to resolving disputes between nations. He believed that diplomacy and compromise, not force, should be employed to bring parties to agreement. Adlai Stevenson was once the governor of Illinois. In 1952 and again in 1956 he headed the Democratic Party and ran for president. Both times Dwight Eisenhower defeated him.

Stevenson favored setting up a conference between Kennedy and Khrushchev. At such a conference, the United States could offer to dismantle its missiles in Turkey in exchange for the USSR moving its weapons out

General Curtis LeMay (right) often encourged President Kennedy
to destroy the Soviet missile sites in Cuba.

of Cuba. At first, Kennedy rejected the missile trade-off suggestion. He thought it would look to the world as if the United States was backing down to Soviet pressure. However, the missiles in Turkey were more than five years old. They were Jupiters, liquid-fueled rockets that required a lengthy fueling process before they could be launched. At the time, Jupiters were considered militarily obsolete, and they were being replaced by the newer Minutemen rockets. The Minutemen missiles could be fired with the push of a button without waiting for the fueling procedure.

At 9:00 P.M. the ExComm team moved from the State Department to the White House to confer with the president. These were important men who were used to being ushered around Washington in private chauffeur-driven limousines. But too many such cars coming and going from the White House would arouse the suspicion of newspaper reporters. So nine men squeezed into one limousine for the quick trip to the White House. Robert Kennedy sat on another man's lap.[12]

The conference resumed at the president's office. The hawks had their say. The doves had their say. Day Three ended with the consensus moving toward a blockade. A blockade represented a blending of the hawk and dove viewpoints. It would start with U.S. naval ships stopping Soviet vessels on the high seas. This was a militarily aggressive move. But, it was hoped, the blockade

The Polaris Missile

The Polaris, America's newest missile at the time, was deployed during the Cuban missile crisis. The Polaris was an intermediate-range rocket that was fired from a submerged submarine. The submarines were almost impossible for an enemy to detect and destroy before the missiles could be fired. The Polaris—perhaps the most unstoppable weapon in any nation's arsenal—was the latest product of the frenzied arms race.

A Polaris A3 fleet ballistic missile lifts off during a test launch from the nuclear-powered strategic missile submarine *F.O.M. Robert E. Lee.*

would force the Soviets to negotiate and let diplomacy resolve the crisis.

Despite the terrible tension surrounding ExComm members, Day Three closed on a note of humor. General Curtis LeMay told the president, "I say, you're in a pretty bad fix." Kennedy answered, "You're in [it] with me."[13] The men around them chuckled.

Day Four: Friday, October 19, 1962

President Kennedy flew to Ohio and later to Illinois. The congressional elections were less than three weeks away. Fellow Democrats were eager to have the president speak on their behalf. Making these routine campaign appearances was important in order to keep the Cuban situation secret. But newspaper reporters have ways of noticing events behind the scenes. Army and Marine units were on the alert in Florida in case the president ordered an invasion of Cuba. Several Florida newspapers had already reported on the increase of military truck columns on the state's highways.

Kennedy gave the appearance that everything was fine in the nation. He had a marvelous way of bringing out the voters during campaign trips. Kennedy was forty-five years old in 1962, youthful compared to recent presidents. He also had movie-star good looks. His beautiful wife and cute kids were darlings in the eyes of the public.

He was a great campaigner, greeting the masses and shaking hands while flashing his famous smile. But as he spoke to the excited crowds in October 1962 his thoughts were probably on Cuba and the Soviet missiles there.

In Washington, ExComm met all day Friday and into Friday night. Robert Kennedy later wrote:

> *The strain and hours without sleep were beginning to take their toll . . . [we experienced] impatience, fit[s] of anger. Each one of us was being asked to make a recommendation which, if wrong and if accepted, could mean the destruction of the human race. That kind of pressure does strange things to a human being.*[14]

ExComm took a vote and the majority recommended a blockade of Cuba. This was a recommendation, nothing more. The final decision lay with President Kennedy.

Chapter 5

You must remember we are dealing with a madman.[1]

> —Diplomat Dean Acheson, giving President Kennedy his opinions of Nikita Khrushchev.

Day Five: Saturday, October 20, 1962

President Kennedy was in a Chicago hotel early in the morning when his brother called. Robert Kennedy told his brother that work on the Cuban missiles was proceeding faster than anyone had anticipated. Also Robert Kennedy said that someone on the White House staff may be leaking information on the Cuban missiles to the press. According to the attorney general, some newspapers were hinting that an air of crisis hung over Washington. This despite the fact that the president had told everyone within his circle to keep the missiles a secret.

The president was due to fly to California that afternoon, but he changed his plans. It was announced that President Kennedy caught a cold and would have to return to Washington for rest. Kennedy was seen leaving his downtown Chicago hotel and getting into a limousine for the ride to the airport. He was wearing a hat, which was unusual for him. Kennedy had thick hair, the envy of many men his age. He mostly went out without a hat. But now he wore a hat because he wanted people to think he had a cold.

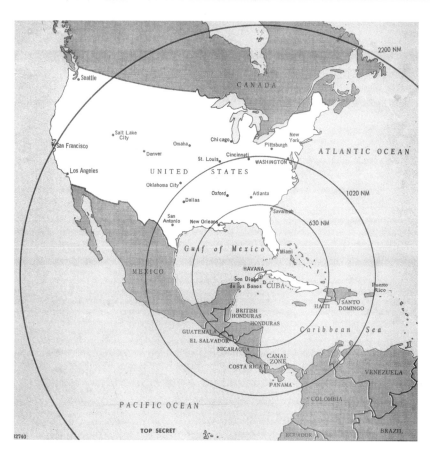

This map shows the range of the Soviet missiles in Cuba. President Kennedy knew that much of the United States could be attacked if the missiles remained in place.

Upon arriving in Washington, the president received distressing news. Intelligence reports claimed that as many as eight Soviet missiles were already operational.[2] Other missiles were being made ready at a rapid pace.

No one knows Kennedy's inner thoughts as he faced this crisis. The coming clash loomed as a duel between him and Soviet premier Khrushchev. At this point, Fidel

Castro was seen as a minor player. The president and his staff believed only Khrushchev had the final authority to fire the Cuban missiles and plunge the world into nuclear war.

Kennedy and Khrushchev came from sharply different backgrounds. While the Soviet leader was born into a family of illiterate peasants, John F. Kennedy was the son of a Boston millionaire banker. His father, Joseph P. Kennedy, had been a friend of President Franklin Roosevelt. Both Kennedy and Khrushchev had seen war firsthand. In World War II, Khrushchev served as a political officer. He preached Communist principals to the men of the Soviet army and made sure the orders of Joseph Stalin were carried out to the letter. Khrushchev was present at Stalingrad, one of the bloodiest battles of that war. Kennedy commanded a small wooden torpedo boat, called a PT, in the Pacific. One night in 1943, his boat was rammed by a Japanese destroyer and sliced in half. The future president became a war hero after he helped rescue the crew. He swam through shark-infested waters while dragging a wounded man behind him.

During the Cuban missile crisis, Kennedy often told the ExComm team that he did not want to put Khrushchev in a corner. He hoped to give the Soviet premier room to maneuver so he could ease his way out of this difficult situation. To act harshly at first, such as launching a surprise air raid on the missile sites, might force Khrushchev to strike back with harshness of his own. Khrushchev could move troops into Berlin. He could bomb the American missile bases in Turkey. Also, some of the missiles in Cuba would probably survive an American air strike. Those remaining missiles could then be fired on U.S. cities with great loss of life.

Robert Kennedy claimed the president made his final decision on Saturday afternoon, Day Five of the crisis.[3] He determined the United States would blockade Cuba to prevent Soviet ships from bringing more missiles to the island. The blockade was not even to be called a blockade because that word sounded too much like an act of war.

Instead, the navy would "quarantine" Cuba. This meant that the navy would only prevent offensive weapons from being shipped to Cuba. Ships would be stopped at sea, inspected, and allowed to pass if they contained only commercial cargo.

The quarantine policy left many issues and questions unresolved. What if ships refused to stop when challenged? What about the missiles already in place on Cuba? What of Berlin, Turkey, and all the other spots in the world where the United Staates was vulnerable to Soviet attack? Dangerous possibilities abounded. But the blockade—called a quarantine—was ordered.

President Kennedy doodled and took notes during a meeting on the Cuban missile crisis. On this page of drawings, the phrase "Blockade Cuba!" is circled.

Day Six: Sunday, October 21, 1962

It was a brilliant fall day in Washington, D.C. Golden sunlight shown on the Mall, the Capitol building, and the statues and monuments, which so delight tourists. On this Sunday afternoon, people around the country watched pro-football games on their black-and-white televisions. (Color TVs were rare in 1962.) Most Americans were comfortable because the early 1960s were years of prosperity. Unemployment was low. Businesses thrived. People generally had a positive outlook about their lives and the future of their children.

But while tourists in the capital enjoyed this fine fall day, the tension inside the White House reached almost unbearable levels.

President Kennedy wrote letters outlining his plans to allies in Europe, Latin America, and Asia. Particularly important was the letter he sent to Mayor Willy Brandt of West Berlin. Kennedy expected some sort of Soviet retaliatory measures on the German city. Letters went out to American embassies around the world warning of the possibility of demonstrations and riots.

Finally a letter went to the Kremlin, the seat of Soviet government in Moscow. Kennedy intended to make a speech to the nation the next day. The speech would announce the quarantine plans. Proper diplomacy required him to inform his adversaries of his coming actions before the national address. Kennedy did not want the Soviet premier to learn of American intentions through watching television, like the rest of the world.

All branches of the armed forces were made ready. Ships went to sea to form a ring around Cuba. Troops relocated to Florida and other southern states in case events called for an invasion of the island. Robert Kennedy later wrote:

> *Missile crews were placed on maximum alert. . . .*
> *[T]he First Armored Division began to move out*
> *of Texas into Georgia, and five more divisions*
> *were placed on the alert. The base at Guantánamo*
> *Bay was strengthened. The Navy deployed one*
> *hundred eighty ships into the Caribbean. . . . The*
> *B-52 bomber force was ordered into the air fully*
> *loaded with atomic weapons. As one came down*
> *to land, another immediately took its place in*
> *the air.*[4]

Reporters easily observed these massive troop movements and guessed the source of the tension was Cuba. The *Washington Post* ran the headline: "Marine Moves in South Linked to Cuban Crisis."[5] The *New York Herald Tribune* said: "Top-Secret Doings in Capital; A Cuban-Berlin Strategy Step?"[6] President Kennedy grew angry at the press speculation. He suspected that someone on his team was "leaking" information to reporters. "This town is a sieve," he complained.[7]

Day Seven: Monday, October 22, 1962

The White House announced the president would address the nation later this night on a matter of grave importance. Before the speech, Kennedy met with key members of Congress to brief them about the missiles in Cuba and his plan for quarantine. One of the senators attending the meeting was Hubert Humphrey of Minnesota. Humphrey had run for president in the Democratic primary elections of 1960 and was defeated by Kennedy. At the end of the briefing, Humphrey was heard to say, "Thank God I am not the President of the United States."[8]

Diplomatic teams got ready. Ambassador Adlai Stevenson prepared to take America's case before the United Nations (UN). The Organization of American States (OAS) would also be called upon to lend its diplomatic efforts to a peaceful resolution of the crisis. The OAS was an association of Latin American countries.

The president was scheduled to make his speech at 7 P.M. Eastern Standard Time. Americans still did not know the precise reason for the address. Speculation in

Secretary of Defense Robert McNamara (left) and Joint Chiefs of Staff Chairman General Maxwell Taylor were two of the members of the ExComm committee who helped President John F. Kennedy make his decision to blockade Cuba.

the press heightened the nation's tension. "A Day of Mystery in D.C.!" reported the *San Francisco Examiner*.[9] "Is Major U.S. Move in Store for Cuba Next" asked the *Miami Herald*.[10] The possible subject of the president's speech was hotly debated. Everyone knew something important was about to happen. But what?

That evening all regular television programs were canceled so the presidential speech could air. Millions of Americans watched as their president's face appeared on their TV screens. Kennedy looked grim:

> *Good evening, my fellow citizens. This government, as promised, has maintained the closest surveillance of the Soviet military buildup on the island of Cuba. Within the past week unmistakable evidence has established the fact that a series of offensive missile sites is now in preparation on that imprisoned island. The purposes of these bases can be none other than to provide a nuclear strike capability against the Western Hemisphere.*

The president then explained what he planned to do about the missiles: "First: . . . a strict quarantine on all offensive military equipment under shipment to Cuba is being initiated. All ships of any kind bound for Cuba from whatever nation or port will, if found to contain cargoes of offensive weapons, be turned back."

In firm but cautious language, the president told the Soviets to quit work on making the missiles operational, or "further action will be justified." Kennedy's third point was particularly significant: "Third: It shall be the policy of this Nation to regard any nuclear missile launched from Cuba against any nation in the Western Hemisphere as an attack by the Soviet Union on the United States, requiring a full retaliatory response upon the Soviet Union." Thus the Soviets—not the Cubans—would be blamed for any missile strike launched from Cuba.

Kennedy called for, "the prompt dismantling and withdrawal of all offensive weapons in Cuba." He appealed to Khrushchev's sense of reason. "He [Khrushchev] has an opportunity now to move the world back from the abyss of destruction—by . . . withdrawing these weapons from Cuba." President Kennedy concluded the speech on a somber note:

> The path we have chosen for the present is full of hazards, as all paths are. . . . The cost of freedom is always high—and Americans have always paid it. . . . Our goal is not the victory of might . . . not peace at the expense of freedom, but both peace and freedom, here in this hemisphere, and, we hope, around the world. God willing, that goal will be achieved.[11]

LIFE

THE DANGER-FILLED WEEK OF DECISION
CUBA

IN BRILLIANT COLOR
The Great Council in Rome

**U.S. NAVY
OFF CUBA**

NOVEMBER 2 · 1962 · 20¢

The cover of the November 2, 1962 *Life* magazine featured a photograph of U.S. Navy warships off the coast of Cuba, accompanied by the headline "The Danger-Filled Week of Decision: Cuba." These ships were there as part of the quarantine.

I have not assumed that you or any other sane man would, in this nuclear age, deliberately plunge the world into war which it is crystal clear no country could win and which could only result in catastrophic consequences to the world, including the aggressor. . . .[1]

—A note written by John F. Kennedy to Khrushchev and delivered on the night of Kennedy's speech

Day Eight: Tuesday, October 23, 1962

On the morning of Day Eight, Secretary of State Dean Rusk woke up in the spare bed in his office. The national emergency compelled him to work late into the night and not go home. In turn, he woke up Undersecretary George Ball, who was sleeping on the couch. Instead of saying, "Good morning," Rusk said, "We have won a considerable victory. You and I are still alive."[2] Such was the atmosphere of impending war and the genuine fear of doomsday that prevailed in Washington.

Far at sea, Soviet ships steamed toward Cuba. Awaiting them were scores of U.S. warships. The light and fast destroyers were to play a prime role in this operation. The plan was for destroyers to approach the Soviet ships, order them to stop, and inspect them. One Russian-speaking officer was placed on each American ship. If the Russian vessels refused to stop, the destroyers would fire a warning shot with their guns. The approaching Soviet ships were all merchant vessels, and it was assumed they carried no heavy guns of their own. If they still failed to halt, the destroyer captains were ordered to fire at their rudders or propellers to disable the ships.[3] Hopefully, there would be little or no loss of life among the crew if U.S. warships had to disable the enemy vessels.

Such confrontations on the high seas were fraught with danger. It was known that Soviet submarines were patrolling the waters off Cuba. The subs were quite capable of sinking an American ship. Neither Khrushchev nor Kennedy wanted war. Nuclear war was insanity. But events could easily spiral out of control. One hotheaded ship commander on either side could do something foolish and set matters snowballing—one shot leading to two shots, to three shots, and so on. In a nightmare scenario, neither Kennedy nor Khrushchev could halt the escalation of violence.

Cuba was virtually under an umbrella of American aircraft. Two of the ships on blockade duty were large aircraft carriers—the *Independence* and the *Enterprise.* Each carrier housed about eighty-five aircraft. The naval aircraft were joined by land-based planes. A total of about 550 fighters and bombers were set to attack Cuba if an air strike were called.[4] Army troops and Marines were gathering at southern ports in preparation for an invasion. All military leaves were canceled.

Fear and tension swept the United States. World War II and the Korean War were still recent memories. But those conflicts were fought on faraway battlefronts. Now the American people faced an impending war where deadly missiles were only a few miles away. Suddenly there was a very real danger of unseen warheads plunging out of the sky. Whole cities might disappear under the great mushroom-shaped clouds that follow an atomic blast.

Still, there was no general panic in the country. Workers reported to their jobs. Students went to school. However, fear was evident. A Columbia University professor who knew President Kennedy wrote him: "The reaction among students here . . . was *qualitatively* different from anything I've ever witnessed before. . . . These kids were literally scared for their lives and were astonished, somehow, that their lives could be risked by an *American* initiative."[5]

At 9:00 A.M., the Organization of American States (OAS) met in an emergency session. Usually this body was suspicious of U.S. policies. Too often the United States had run roughshod over its Latin American neighbors. But in the Cuban crisis, all Western Hemisphere countries felt threatened by nuclear weapons. The OAS voted overwhelmingly to condemn the Soviet missiles based in Cuba.

At noon, Kennedy received a cabled letter from Moscow. It was the first official Soviet reaction to the quarantine. The letter denounced the quarantine as a violation of international law. Several members of the Kennedy team pointed out that the quarantine was consistent with the Monroe Doctrine. However, the president did not want to invoke the principles of the Monroe

Secretary of Defense Dean Rusk addresses an emergency meeting of the Organization of American States on October 23, 1962, in Washington. He asked the group to back President Kennedy's blockade of Cuba.

Doctrine. In the past, the Monroe Doctrine had been used as an excuse to invade Latin American nations. Kennedy wanted Latin American unity as he pressured the Soviets to withdraw from Cuba. The OAS vote affirmed he had, at least for a time, achieved that unity.

Meanwhile, Soviet merchant vessels steamed steadily toward U.S. warships. A confrontation with the possibility of terrible consequences was hours away. The last line of the Khrushchev letter to Kennedy was significant. The Soviet chief offered to meet with the American president and discuss a peaceful solution. However, he warned that "if the United States insists on war [then] we'll all meet in hell."[6]

Day Nine: Wednesday, October 24, 1962

According to Robert Kennedy:

> *This Wednesday-morning meeting . . . seemed the most trying, the most difficult and the most filled with tension. The Russian ships were proceeding . . . and we either had to intercept them or announce we were withdrawing. I sat across the table from the President. . . . The danger and concern that we all felt hung like a cloud over us all and particularly over the President.*[7]

Remembering the Crisis

The author of this book was a college junior at the Champaign–Urbana campus of the University of Illinois in 1962. Central Illinois was a rural area, and it did not seem to be a likely target for nuclear missiles. Yet the author remembers concern shown by students and faculty members. Many people in the community hoarded food.

One of the author's friends was a newly married man who lived in Chicago. The friend gathered his family in an old car and drove miles away to a farming region in Wisconsin to escape possible nuclear attack. Later, the author discussed this move with his friend. The author believed the postnuclear war world would be a horrible place in which to live. Survivors of the initial bombings might very well die slowly of radiation sickness. Wouldn't it be better simply to get killed in the initial exchange of bombs? The subject made for interesting discussions. All around the country, similar conversations were taking place.

There always loomed the fear that one miscalculation, one wrong move, could plunge the world into war. President Kennedy labored to keep the situation under his control. Was such control possible? He and his team sat in offices in the White House. Hundreds of miles away, on the high seas, ships were about to confront other ships. No one in the White House was able to supervise or in any way regulate events about to take place on the ocean. Accidental war stood out as the possible nightmare that haunted the minds of everyone involved in the crisis.

Stores around the country reported a rush of customers buying canned goods. People reasoned that canned food would serve as emergency rations in the event of an air raid. Police stations were flooded with calls: Where is the city's air-raid shelter? How much warning will we get? Are the Russians going to invade? Will they bomb us?

Fear was especially prevalent in Florida and the southeastern states. Long military truck columns rumbled over highways in the South, adding to the urgent sense of war. The trucks towed artillery pieces and tanks on flatbed trailers. Hotels in the southeast experienced a rash of cancellations. Vacationers from the cold states up north decided to stay home this winter. With war pending, a vacation in the sunny south was simply not worth the risk.

At ten in the morning, Secretary of Defense McNamara made an important announcement to the ExComm meeting. Radio reports said the American fleet was about to make its first interception. Two Russian ships were just a few miles away from American destroyers. The ships were in radio contact with Moscow. The ExComm men believed the Soviet vessels were under direct orders from the Kremlin. Would the enemy ships stop when commanded? Or were the vessels under orders to defy the quarantine?

Adding to the tension, Secretary McNamara learned a Soviet submarine patrolled the waters near the two merchant ships.

"Isn't there some way we can avoid having our first exchange with a Russian submarine—almost anything but that," said President Kennedy.

"No," answered McNamara, "there's too much danger to our ships. There is no alternative."[8]

Robert Kennedy looked across the conference table to his brother. He later wrote about this tense moment: "I think these few minutes were the time of gravest concern for the President. Was the world on the brink of a holocaust? Was it our error? A mistake? [The president's] hand went up to his face and covered his mouth. His face seemed drawn, his eyes pained, almost gray."[9]

At 10:25 the meeting was interrupted by a messenger who handed a letter to John McCone, a member of ExComm. "Mr. President," McCone said, "we have a

U.S. Secretary of Defense Robert S. McNamara informed the rest of the ExComm members about the first possible interception of Soviet ships by the U.S. naval blockade.

preliminary report which seems to indicate that some of the Russian ships have stopped dead in the water."[10]

A hush that lasted several minutes overcame the meeting. Robert Kennedy checked the clock. It was 10:32 A.M.

John McCone broke the silence. "The report is accurate, Mr. President," said McCone. "Six ships previously on their way to Cuba at the edge of the quarantine line have stopped or have turned back toward the Soviet Union."[11]

President Kennedy then told his naval aide to radio all American warships. They were not to pursue the retreating Russian vessels. As a navy veteran who had been in combat, the president knew about armed clashes at sea. He wanted to avoid any kind of a sea battle at this point. He insisted U.S. warships give the Soviets plenty of room to return home.

Secretary of State Dean Rusk then made a famous and often-quoted remark to fellow members of ExComm. The secretary compared the United States and USSR standoff to a fight between two schoolboys. He said, "We are eyeball to eyeball, and I think the other fellow just blinked."[12]

The meeting continued. The immediate crisis of a confrontation at sea had been averted. The relief felt by all ExComm members was overwhelming. The first direct confrontation between the two nuclear superpowers had ended. And the other fellow had blinked.

Chapter 7

Our best judgement is that they [the Soviet leaders] are scratching their brains *very hard* at the present time, deciding just exactly how they want to play this.[1]

—Secretary of State Dean Rusk

Day Ten: Thursday, October 25, 1962

Most of the Russian vessels heading for Cuba had either stopped or turned around and went home. Why? Did Khrushchev want to end this crisis peacefully? Or was he just buying time? Dozens of missiles remained in Cuba. Work on making those missiles operational continued at a rapid pace. The potentially deadly confrontation between the two superpowers was far from over.

The U.S. Air Force prepared for war. The Strategic Air Command (SAC) raised its alert status to Defcon-2. SAC was the nation's bomber force. Its prime mission was to drop nuclear bombs on enemy targets. There were five levels of Defense Readiness Condition (Defcon) alerts. Defcon-1 was all-out war. Defcon-2 was one step away from war. Never before or since in the long history of the Cold War did the alert status reach the level of Defcon-2.[2] The advanced Defcon alert meant that nuclear bombs were loaded onto giant SAC bombers and made ready for use at a moment's notice.[3] American crews manning ballistic missiles armed with nuclear warheads also went on high alert.

Fear continued its grip on the American people. Highways in Florida swarmed with military traffic. Miami telephone companies claimed long-distance calls were up 25 percent.[4] Officials in the New York City school system ordered air-raid drills. The drills frightened many children.

Americans pray for peace during the Cuban missile crisis.

At sea, a few Russian ships continued to advance toward Cuba. American destroyers closed in on those vessels. The first actual intercept of a Soviet cargo craft took place on Day Ten. At 8:00 A.M., the American destroyer *Gearing* approached the Soviet tanker *Bucharest* and ordered it to stop. Over the radio, the tanker captain said his ship carried only petroleum products. The exchange between the two ships was radioed to the ExComm team in Washington where decisions on enforcing the quarantine were being made. Kennedy's men decided to let the *Bucharest* go without boarding the vessel. They reasoned it was unlikely a tanker would carry missiles.

This first intercept, though it was uneventful, triggered a debate among the ExComm members. Many members believed the quarantine ought to be stepped up and made to apply to all goods heading toward Cuba. The Russians were making rapid progress to complete all their missile sites. So why not cut off their supplies? A shortage of any product, such as petroleum to fuel trucks, could slow the Soviet technicians. The arguments raged at ExComm meetings, but the scope of the quarantine was never expanded.

The drama of Day Ten shifted to New York City and the United Nations (UN) An emergency UN session was called to discuss a peaceful solution to the crisis, which had the whole world in an uproar. Providing a format for debate was a major function of the world body. On the floor of the UN, adversary nations could battle with words instead of weapons.

Adlai Stevenson, the American ambassador, stood before the assembly of nations. Stevenson was an elegant speaker and known to be a mild-mannered and gentlemanly individual. He often sounded more like a college professor than a political leader. Today he faced Ambassador Valerian Zorin, the Soviet delegate. Zorin had claimed repeatedly that there were no Soviet offensive missiles in Cuba. Today, the normally good-tempered Stevenson was feisty.

"Do you, Ambassador Zorin," Stevenson said, "deny that the U.S.S.R. has placed and is placing medium- and intermediate-range ballistic missiles and sites in Cuba?"

Zorin hesitated as if waiting to hear the translation over his earphones. Yet he spoke English well, and Stevenson thought he was simply stalling.

"Yes or no," snapped Stevenson, "don't wait for the translation—yes or no?"

Zorin said, "I am not in an American courtroom, sir, and therefore I do not wish to answer. . . ."

Stevenson interrupted him, "You are in the courtroom of world opinion right now, and you can answer yes or no."

U.S. Ambassador Adlai Stevenson addresses the U.N. Security Council during a session at the United Nations headquarters in New York on October 23, 1962.

UNITED STATES

"You will have your answer in due course," said Ambassador Zorin.

"I am prepared to wait for my answer until hell freezes over," said Stevenson.[5]

Ambassador Stevenson then motioned to an aide. A large photo propped up by an easel was brought before the assembly. It was a picture taken from an American reconnaissance plane, and it clearly showed a Soviet missile site. Presenting this reconnaissance photo was a dramatic move on Stevenson's part. Before the entire world, Stevenson exposed Zorin as a liar.

Millions watched this UN debate on television. One of those watching was President Kennedy. "Terrific," said Kennedy when Stevenson produced the photo. "I never knew Adlai had it in him. Too bad he didn't show some of this steam in the 1956 campaign."[6] Kennedy was referring to the rather bland presidential contest that Stevenson waged, and lost, for the Democratic Party in 1956.

Day Eleven: Friday, October 26, 1962

Early in the morning, another ship heading for Cuba was stopped by American destroyers. It was the *Marucla*, a Lebanese freighter manned by a Greek crew and leased by the USSR. One of the destroyers stopping the vessel was the DD850, the *Joseph P. Kennedy Jr.* That destroyer was named after President Kennedy's older brother, who was killed in World War II. In August 1944, Joseph P. Kennedy, Jr., a naval pilot, volunteered to fly a dangerous bombing mission against a German target. His aircraft exploded in mid-flight, killing Kennedy and his copilot. In 1946, the destroyer DD850 was named in honor of the war hero and Kennedy brother.

A team of American sailors boarded the *Marucla* to inspect its cargo. The scene was almost comic. One American officer spoke Russian, but the captain of the *Marucla* was a Greek. None of the Americans spoke the Greek language. So the men communicated using hand gestures. The captain, who was in a good mood, served the Americans coffee while they looked around. They found nothing suspicious and left the ship. This event was largely a demonstration. ExComm members doubted that the Russians would put offensive weapons on a foreign flag ship. But the Kennedy team wanted to prove to the Soviet leaders that the U.S. Navy could and would board one of their vessels.[7]

October 26 marked the fourth day after the Kennedy speech, which announced the presence of Soviet missiles on Cuban soil. The newscaster Chet Huntley called that presidential address, "the toughest and the most grim speech by a president since December 7, 1941, when President Roosevelt spoke to the Congress and the nation about the day of infamy . . . the attack on Pearl Harbor."[8]

The Kennedy speech sent a wave of fear tearing through the country. That fear magnified as the crisis progressed. All the nations' attention focused on the White House. At any minute, the president could order an air strike, an invasion, or both on Cuba. Such a move could escalate into atomic war. *Newsweek* magazine reported: "Throughout the nation Americans hung by their radios and TV sets. . . . There was the gnawing apprehension everywhere that this time might really be it."[9]

One of the newsmen keeping the country informed was John Scali of ABC television. He covered the State Department and had friends in that agency. The tense international situation was keeping him and all the other newscasters busy. Instead of taking a leisurely lunch, Scali ate a bologna sandwich at his desk. Suddenly his phone rang. It was Aleksandr Fomin, the official public-affairs officer for the Soviet Embassy. It is unclear exactly why the Soviets approached Scali at this time instead of someone closer to President Kennedy. But this first contact ultimately produced a diplomatic breakthrough. Fomin suggested that he and Scali meet for lunch right away. Scali knew that Fomin was not his real name and that his work in public affairs was a cover-up. His real name was Alexander Feklisov and he was a Soviet spy.[10]

At lunch, Fomin told Scali the situation was very serious and that "war seems about to break out."[11] He asked if the United States would be receptive to a deal.

Picketers representing an organization known as Women Strike for Peace carry signs outside the United Nations headquarters in New York City where the U.N. Security Council considered the Cuban missile crisis.

The USSR would withdraw its missiles in exchange for a U.S. pledge not to invade Cuba. Scali said he did not know if American leaders would approve of such a deal. However, he knew Fomin was a high Soviet official and he reasoned that this proposal would have to come from top leaders in Moscow. Scali contacted his friends in the State Department.

From the beginning of the crisis, Kennedy and Khrushchev had been exchanging letters, which came as cablegrams (long-distance telegrams that transmitted messages in those days). Many of Khrushchev's cablegrams were extensive and tended to ramble. But he repeatedly said that nuclear war was madness. Like Kennedy, he expressed the fear that war could break out despite the efforts of the two leaders to stop it. In one letter he said:

> *[We] ought not now to pull on the ends of the rope in which you have tied the knot of war, because the more the two of us pull, the tighter that knot will be tied. And the moment may come when that knot will be tied so tight that even he who tied it will not have the strength to untie it.[12]*

Yet none of Khrushchev's letters or cablegrams contained an idea or a specific plan suggesting how to defuse the dangerous nuclear standoff. The proposal by Fomin to Scali might be the germ of such a plan.

At six in the afternoon (1:00 A.M. Moscow time), a letter arrived from Khrushchev via teletype. Again it was long and emotional. But for the first time Khrushchev admitted he had offensive missiles in Cuba. He also repeated the Fomin plan. "This is my proposal," the Soviet leader said. "No more weapons to Cuba and those within Cuba withdrawn or destroyed, and you reciprocate by withdrawing your blockade and also agree not to invade Cuba."[13]

The letter broke new ground and was perhaps a vital first step in peacefully resolving the crisis. Robert Kennedy later wrote, "I had a slight feeling of optimism as I drove home from the State Department that night. The letter, with all its rhetoric, had the beginnings perhaps of some accommodation, some agreement." [14]

It is not clear if the Soviets told Castro or other Cuban leaders about their offer to Kennedy. At this stage in the crisis, the proposals and counterproposals were exchanged only between the two superpowers. The fate of Cuba was a minor consideration when weighed against the possibility of World War III. Fidel Castro could do little to impose his will on the two larger nations.

Meanwhile, the United States remained in a state of high anxiety. The missile crisis was on everyone's mind, and it dominated conversations between friends and neighbors. Americans were nervous, on edge, and fearful. In Jacksonville, Florida, an air-raid siren accidentally sounded, and the city's police department was flooded with forty thousand phone calls.[15]

Chapter 8

If indeed war should break out, then it would not be in our power to stop it, for such is the logic of war. I have participated in two wars and know that war ends when it has rolled through cities and villages, everywhere sowing death and destruction.[1]

> —From a letter written by Nikita Khrushchev to John F. Kennedy at the height of the Cuban missile crisis.

Day Twelve: Saturday, October 27, 1962

Day Twelve began with a near catastrophe at sea. Several U.S. destroyers pursued the Soviet submarine B-59. The submarine was underwater. The destroyers tried to force it to surface. The Americans did not know the sub was experiencing engine problems. The B-59 was powered by a diesel-electric motor. When below the surface, it ran on batteries. Now the batteries were giving out. Temperatures inside the sub soared to more than 100 degrees Fahrenheit. Several crewmen fainted due to heat and foul air.[2]

The submarine commander, Captain Valentin Savitski, grew furious with the actions of the U.S. destroyers. Included in his arsenal was one torpedo armed with a small nuclear warhead.[3] Such a torpedo could obliterate any U.S. ship and kill everyone on board. According to a

Russian account, Captain Savitski screamed at fellow officers, "We're going to blast them now! We will die, but we will sink them all—we will not disgrace our Navy."[4]

Other officers persuaded Savitski to bring the sub to the surface. Once surfaced, the Russians exchanged signals of peace with the Americans. A jazz band played on the deck of the U.S. destroyer *Cony* and perhaps the music helped to sooth tempers.[5] The B-59 repaired its engines and sailed away on the surface. This dangerous encounter at sea went unnoticed in the United States for decades until a Russian journalist published the story. It was exactly the type of incident that both Kennedy and Khrushchev feared most. One hot-tempered commander came close to touching off a wave of events that could have snowballed into nuclear war.

Day Twelve brought tragedy in the air above Cuba. A Soviet missile shot down a U-2 flown by Major Rudolf Anderson, Jr., from South Carolina. Anderson was killed. The news was greeted with shock and gloom by the ExComm team. Everyone felt sorry for Anderson and his family. But this also meant the Soviet Surface to Air Missiles (SAMs) were operational. President Kennedy said, "How can we send any more U-2 pilots into this area tomorrow unless we take out all of the SAM sites? We are now in an entirely new ball game."[6]

The death of Major Anderson dashed the hopeful mood that prevailed with the Kennedy team after the Scali

American destroyers pursued a Soviet submarine on October 27, 1962, during the Cuban missile crisis. Above is a modern-day destroyer, the U.S.S. *Porter*.

and Fomin exchange and the Khrushchev letter. Also they learned that personnel in the Soviet Embassy in Washington were destroying all their sensitive records.[7] Such destruction of paper records was often a final step before war. Gloom gripped ExComm. Once more the world seemed to be at the brink of destruction. Robert Kennedy noted: "There was the realization that the Soviet Union and Cuba apparently were preparing to do battle. And there was the feeling that the noose was tightening on all of us . . . that the bridges to escape were crumbling."[8]

Adding to the atmosphere of despair was a second letter from Khrushchev. This letter was broadcast by radio to the Russian people. It brought a new demand to the table: The United States must agree to withdraw its missiles from Turkey before the Soviet Union dismantled its weapons in Cuba.

The demand for a missile trade-off presented the Kennedy team with a dilemma, a choice between two bad alternatives. The missiles in Turkey were obsolete Jupiter types. Plans had already been made to remove the Jupiters from Turkish soil. But could the United States take them away now in the face of Soviet pressure? ExComm feared such a move would give the appearance of weakness. On the one hand, it seemed stupid to risk war over a few obsolete missiles based in Turkey. But this was gamesmanship on a frightening scale. Friends and allies around the world would lose respect for the United States if it gave ground in this nuclear game of chicken.

On all fronts, the situation worsened by the hour. Reports from Cuba said the Soviets were working day and night to get all the missiles operational. Top American generals recommended the United States launch an air strike on Monday, followed by an invasion. Robert Kennedy said of Day Twelve, "[These were] the most difficult twenty-four hours of the missile crisis."[9]

Finally the ExComm men decided on a response to Khrushchev's letter. It was a chance—perhaps a last chance—to avert war. Robert Kennedy later wrote: "I suggested . . . that we ignore the latest Khrushchev letter and respond [only] to his earlier [one]."[10] President Kennedy wrote a letter that agreed to the earlier proposal: The United States pledged not to invade Cuba in exchange for a Soviet withdrawal of its missiles. The Cuba-Turkey trade-off was simply ignored. The letter was sent by cable. Would this ploy work? Would Khrushchev insist on the removal of missiles from Turkey and thus give the appearance of a United States defeat? Everyone waited for the Soviet reaction.

The ExComm meeting on Day Twelve broke up at about 7:30 P.M. Years later, Defense Secretary McNamara said, "I remember the sunset. We left at about the time the sun was setting in October, and I, at least, was so uncertain [about the future] . . . that I wondered if I'd ever see another sunset like that."[11]

Day Thirteen: Sunday, October 28, 1962

On this Sunday morning, church attendance was up by 20 percent across the country.[12] In New York, the largest peace demonstration ever seen in that city assembled in front of the UN building. People prayed for peace. People demanded peace.

The military prepared for war. The alert status for the Strategic Air Command remained at Defcon-2. Planes were readied to bomb Cuba in twenty-four hours. Five million pamphlets were printed up warning Cuban civilians to take cover.[13] The pamphlets were to be dropped before the actual bombs. Soldiers and Marines were massed along the Florida coast, armed for invasion. More than one hundred naval vessels crowded the coastal waters in anticipation of a landing on Cuban beaches.[14] These vast forces were poised to spring into action at the command of one man—President John F. Kennedy.

That morning, Kennedy dressed to go to church. The radio in his bedroom played popular music. The music stopped abruptly as an announcer told listeners to stand by for an important news bulletin. Kennedy was the most powerful man in the world. Yet that morning he heard the news of the world's fate the same way as practically every other person—over the radio. At 9:00 A.M. Washington time (6:00 P.M. Moscow time) a spokesman in Moscow broadcast a new letter from Khrushchev to Kennedy: "In order to complete with greater speed the liquidation of the conflict dangerous to the cause of peace . . . [I have] issued a new order on the dismantling of the weapons which you describe as 'offensive,' and their crating and return to the Soviet Union."[15]

Khrushchev said he would immediately remove Russian missiles in exchange for a U.S. pledge not to invade Cuba. The ploy had worked. In his letter, Kennedy avoided the sticky problems associated with a Cuba-Turkey missile trade by simply not mentioning the trade. This letter from Khrushchev did not mention the trade either.

To the relief of the entire world, the Cuban missile crisis was over. On that Sunday morning, men and women around the globe celebrated peace and freedom from fear.

Only a handful of people were aware of a silent agreement made between the United States and the USSR. The night before Day Thirteen, Robert Kennedy had met with Soviet Ambassador Anatoly Dobrynin in Washington. At the meeting, Robert Kennedy said the U.S. missiles in Turkey and Italy would soon be removed as a matter of course. Robert Kennedy later wrote: "I said [to Dobrynin], President Kennedy had been anxious to remove those missiles . . . for a long period of time."[16]

An informal deal was struck. The United States would remove its missiles from the Soviet Union's doorstep, but the removal would not be considered a trade for those in Cuba. The Jupiter missiles in Turkey and Italy were old devices, which had lost their military value. They would simply be retired. Robert Kennedy was careful to put nothing in writing concerning the Jupiters. He simply gave his word that the Turkish missiles would soon be gone. Five months later, the Jupiters were, indeed,

The front page of the *New York Times* for October 29, 1962, announces the Soviet Union's agreement to remove its guided missiles from Cuba.

withdrawn from Turkey and Italy. Government leaders in Turkey objected, but the removal drew scant attention from the world press.

On the evening of Day Thirteen, President Kennedy watched the televised news program, *Washington Report*, which was broadcast live over CBS. Sitting at his side was Press Secretary Pierre Salinger. Finally, the president could relax. Reports from Cuba claimed Russian technicians had already started disassembling the missiles. On the television news show, two newsmen hailed the ending of the Cuban missile crisis as a victory for the United States.

"Tell them to stop that," Kennedy told Salinger.

Salinger called the CBS studios and spoke to one of the newsmen, David Schoenbrun:

David, I'm speaking from the Oval Office. The President is right next to me. Please do not . . . run on about a Soviet defeat. Do not play this up as a victory for us. There is a danger that Khrushchev will be so humiliated and angered that he will change his mind. . . . Do not mess this up for us.[17]

Not even the president had the power to tell these men how they should report the news. Such is the nature of free-speech laws in the United States. But the newsmen did as Salinger advised.

U.S. Navy Patrol P 3V-1 flies over a missile-carrying
Soviet ship, *Potzunov*, as it leaves Cuba after the
Cuban missile crisis had been averted.

Chapter 9

It is insane that two men, sitting on opposite sides of the world, should be able to decide to bring an end to civilization.[1]

> —President John F. Kennedy commenting on the Cuban missile crisis

[W]e had installed enough missiles already to destroy New York, Chicago, and the other huge industrial cities, not to mention a little village like Washington.[2]

> —Premier Nikita Khrushchev, writing in the late 1960s

Immediate Reactions to the Settlement

Fidel Castro was furious. The Cuban chief believed Khrushchev and the Soviet leaders had betrayed him. Throughout the tense days of negotiation between Kennedy and Khrushchev, his opinions had been ignored. Castro wanted desperately to keep the missiles in Cuba, even at the risk of a U.S. invasion. Now he felt disgraced and humiliated by the Soviet pullback. The decision left him weakened and alone, as he was before he agreed to let the Soviets put their missiles on Cuban soil. Yes, the Cuban leader had an American pledge not to launch an outright invasion on his island nation. But the Americans were free to encourage anti-Communist Cubans to revolt against the present

U.S. President John F. Kennedy reports to the nation on the status of the Cuban missile crisis on November 2, 1962. He told radio and television listeners that Soviet missile bases "are being destroyed."

government. An angry Fidel Castro wrote Khrushchev: "Countless eyes of Cuban and Soviet men who were willing to die with supreme dignity shed tears upon learning about the surprising, sudden and practically unconditional decision to withdraw the weapons."[3]

Castro finally imposed his own partial will on the settlement. The Soviet Union had agreed to allow UN inspectors to come to its weapons sites to ensure that all the missiles had been removed. Castro refused to permit the inspectors to enter Cuba. Instead, the missiles were lashed to the decks of Soviet ships, and an American aircraft photographed them from above. President Kennedy seemed pleased with the Soviet solution. He made no vigorous effort to force the inspection issue.

For his part, Nikita Khrushchev told the world he had won a victory in Cuba. He devoted only a short chapter of his memoirs to the Cuban missile crisis. The Soviet leader said he put the missiles in Cuba in order to safeguard that island nation from a U.S. invasion. He now had a pledge from the United States not to invade. Therefore, the missiles had served their purpose and were no longer needed. Khrushchev wrote: "The [Cuban missile crisis] was a triumph of Soviet foreign policy and a personal triumph in my own career as a statesman. . . . We achieved, I would say, a spectacular success without having to fire a single shot."[4]

Several American generals were upset with the Cuban settlement. Many believed the Soviets were hiding missiles somewhere on Cuban soil. Other military men had wanted to invade Cuba in order to stamp out a Communist government operating so close to U.S. shores. Angriest of all was the U.S. Air Force chief Curtis E. LeMay. Banging his hand on a table, LeMay said the settlement was "the greatest defeat in our history." He shouted at Kennedy, "We should invade today!"[5]

The Soviet freighter, *Bonronec*, sails away from Havana, Cuba, on November 9, 1962. The photo shows a close-up of mobile missile launchers covered with a tarp.

President Kennedy was shocked by LeMay's outburst. He later remarked to Robert McNamara that he felt a closeness with Khrushchev because the Soviet leader probably had "to cope with a Curtis LeMay of his own."[6]

The American people felt a sense of relief and victory after the missiles were taken away. All apparent signs said the Soviets backed down under the U.S. threat of force.

The promise to remove missiles from Turkey and Italy was not made public. The U.S. pledge not to invade Cuba was announced, but that seemed to be a minor concession. Most Americans believed their country faced the crisis bravely and won the day.

Election Day came on November 6, 1962. Kennedy's Democratic Party did very well. Certainly the country was prosperous and the economy expanding in 1962. But perhaps the Democrats' strong showing came because Americans were pleased with President Kennedy's performance during the missile crisis. The Democrats increased their majority in Congress. Kennedy's youngest brother, Edward, won a seat as U.S. Senator from Massachusetts. The mood of the country was positive. Peace prevailed.

U-2 aircraft continued to fly over Cuba surveying the now-vacated missile sites. The Cuban army had anti-aircraft guns, but it could not hit the high-flying planes. Soviet forces, armed with anti-aircraft missiles, could have knocked down the U-2s. But the Russians were under orders from Moscow not to fire at the American airplanes.[7] President Kennedy held a news conference on December 10, 1962. He told reporters that U-2 photos and other intelligence indicated all Soviet offensive missiles and bombers had been withdrawn from Cuba. Now it was official. The Cuban missile crisis was over.

A Thaw in the Cold War

The Cuban missile crisis brought the world closer to nuclear annihilation than it had ever been before. For thirteen days, the fate of the world—perhaps the lives of everyone on the planet—rested in a delicate balance. Worst of all possible scenarios, a catastrophic war could have broken out despite the efforts of the American and

The U.S. Navy destroyer *Barry* maneuvers about the Russian freighter *Anosov* (left) in the Atlantic Ocean, to inspect its cargo during the Cuban blockade on November 10, 1962. The Soviet ship carried a cargo of missiles being withdrawn from Cuba.

Soviet leaders to stop the violence. Neither side wanted to see world tension reach such perilous heights again.

The confrontation between the two nuclear super-powers and the fear it generated throughout the world ushered in a major thaw in the Cold War. On June 10, 1963, eight months after the crisis, President Kennedy gave a speech to the graduating class of American University in Washington, D.C. The president told the graduates:

> *I have chosen this time and place to discuss a topic*
> *on which too often ignorance abounds. . . . I speak*
> *of peace . . . in an age when a single nuclear*
> *weapon contains almost ten times the explosive*
> *force delivered by all the allied air forces in the*
> *Second World War . . . an age when the deadly*
> *poisons produced by a nuclear exchange would*
> *be carried by wind and water and soil and seed*
> *to the far corners of the globe and to generations*
> *yet unborn. . . .*[8]

President Kennedy urged Americans to take a fresh view of their rival nation. He said:

> *Let us reexamine our attitude toward the Soviet*
> *Union. As Americans we find Communism*
> *profoundly repugnant. . . . But we can still hail the*

Fate of the Principal Figures

President John F. Kennedy was shot and killed by an assassin on November 22, 1963, while he was in Dallas, Texas. The country and the world were shocked by his loss.

Soviet rivals in October 1964 forced Nikita Khrushchev out of his leadership position. It is possible the loss of prestige the Russians suffered by withdrawing their missiles from Cuba was a major reason for his fall from power. Khrushchev died in 1971 at the age of seventy-seven.

A gunman assassinated then-U.S. Senator Robert Kennedy in June 1968. At the time of his death, Robert Kennedy was campaigning for the presidency, an office he might have won had he lived.

Fidel Castro lasted the longest of all the Cuban missile crisis principals. He remained in power in Cuba. In early 2007, Castro, nearing eighty, was reported to be gravely ill and his brother Raúl was leading the nation.

This photo was taken only minutes before President John F. Kennedy was assassinated on November 22, 1963. In the back seat are Kennedy and his wife, Jackie. In the front are Texas Governor John Connolly and his wife, Nellie.

Russian people for their many achievements. . . .
In the final analysis, our most basic common link
is that we all inhabit this small planet. We all
breathe the same air. We all cherish our children's
future. And we are all mortal. . . . Our problems
are man-made—therefore, they can be solved by
man. And man can be as big as he wants.[9]

Still speaking to the graduates, Kennedy announced the United States would not begin a new round of atomic-bomb tests that were scheduled to take place in the atmosphere. Such above-ground tests poison the air. He also said Soviet, British, and American negotiators would soon meet to discuss a treaty banning all atmospheric nuclear testing.

The American University speech led to the Limited Test Ban Treaty, which took effect later in 1963. Terms of the treaty said that the United States, the Soviet Union, and Great Britain would never again test nuclear weapons in the atmosphere. Underground testing was allowed. Other countries, as they developed nuclear weapons, did test them in the atmosphere, however.

In August 1963, the United States and the Soviet Union installed a "hotline," which connected Moscow and Washington. This was years before the Internet and satellite telephones made country-to-country communication easy. During the Cuban missile crisis, it took hours for the two leaders to exchange letters through cablegrams. Now there was a direct telephone line between Washington and Moscow. Future leaders could simply pick up the phone and talk to one another. It was hoped the hotline telephone connection could prevent accidental nuclear war.

Despite the Cold War thaw, the arms race continued at its old blistering pace. The U.S. missiles withdrawn from Turkey were replaced by Polaris missiles housed in submarines that patrolled the Mediterranean Sea. The Soviet Union concentrated its efforts on building ICBMs. The ICBMs, based on Soviet soil, could hit targets in the United States. By the end of the 1960s, the Soviets had more ICBMs than did the Americans.[10] The United States, in turn, developed a method of putting several

President Kennedy gave this calendar to all the staff involved with the Cuban missile crisis meetings in 1962. The calendar shows the days October 16–28 in bold type.

warheads on one missile. Sadly, the world remained under a doomsday trigger.

What If?

What if in October 1962 the United States had bombed the Russian missile bases in Cuba? What would have happened if American forces had invaded that island nation? History is loaded with "what if?" questions such as these. Of course, we cannot know for certain the outcome of any act that did not actually take place. But as time passes, we learn more details about contemplated actions. In the case of Cuba, the "what if?" queries are chilling.

Certainly any U.S. action would have started with an air raid on the Cuban missile bases. At first, the U.S. planes would use conventional "iron bombs," not nuclear ones. Virtually all the generals and military advisers told Kennedy that air strikes alone could not destroy all the missiles. Speaking for the military, General Maxwell Taylor advised Kennedy that bombing with conventional bombs would "never be 100 percent"[11] effective.

Therefore, U.S. soldiers and Marines would have to invade Cuba's shores. What kind of forces would they face? At the time of the crisis, the Soviet Union had about forty-two thousand soldiers in Cuba.[12] This number was far greater than U.S. intelligence estimates of Soviet strength. American invaders would also have had to fight

Cuban troops. It was not known how loyal the Cuban army was to Castro or if Cuban soldiers would fight with spirit for the cause of Communism. The Cuban army of today is loyal to its government and is an effective fighting force.

The most terrifying "what if?" possibility involved Russian tactical nuclear weapons. These are small nuclear

President Kennedy (second from left) and advisers confer after an ExComm meeting. These men, and the other ExComm members, worked hard to prevent nuclear war during those fateful thirteen days in October 1962.

warheads intended for battlefield use. Tactical nuclear weapons were delivered in the form of aerial bombs or by short-range rockets. At the planning stage for invasion, U.S. leaders did not know if the Soviets had tactical nuclear weapons in Cuba. We know now the tactical weapons were there and ready for use. Written instructions to the Soviet commander in Cuba, General Issa Pliyev, declared, "In a situation of an enemy landing on the island of Cuba . . . you are permitted to make your own decision and to use the nuclear means [employ tactical nuclear weapons] in order to achieve the complete destruction of the invaders on the Cuban territory and to defend the Republic of Cuba."[13]

The Soviet general did not have the authority to fire the longer-range missiles onto targets in the United States. That authority was reserved for leaders in Moscow. But, as his written orders suggest, tactical weapons were another matter. He was free to fire tactical atomic warheads. Pliyev was a veteran of many bloody battles during World War II. He knew the Americans would enjoy air superiority and could bring scores of tanks and artillery pieces to the island. Therefore, he could easily conclude, his only chance of stopping a U.S. invasion would be to strike back with tactical nuclear weapons.

Tactical atomic weapons used against troops massed on landing beaches would result in battlefield deaths on a scale never seen before. Thousands of soldiers and the ships and crews off shore could be destroyed in an instant. Such a devastating blow would almost have to call for a nuclear response from the Americans. In the height of such an intense war, one desperate act leads to another. One bomb prompts the use of another. It was as if the fate of the world stood like a row of dominoes. One domino is pushed over and hits another, which topples into another and another. The last domino triggers all-out nuclear war. It almost happened in October 1962.

Saner heads triumphed, and a devastating nuclear exchange was averted. Leaders in the United States and the Soviet Union reasoned together, made compromises, and pulled the world from the brink of war. After thirteen days of incredible tension, peace came at last.

TIMELINE

1945—World War II officially ends on September 2 when Japan signs the surrender documents.

1946—Winston Churchill makes his famous Iron Curtain speech at Fulton, Missouri; historians often cite the speech as the beginning of the Cold War.

1948—On June 24, the Russian army blockades West Berlin, forcing the Americans and their allies to supply the city by air in an operation called the Berlin Airlift.

1949—A Communist government takes over in China.

1950—Communist North Korea invades capitalist South Korea, and the Korean War, a "hot" chapter in the cold war, breaks out.

1953—A cease-fire is declared, ending the fighting in the Korean War after terrible death and destruction.

1957—On October 4, the USSR announces the launching of *Sputnik I*, history's first human-made earth satellite; the launching serves as evidence that the Soviets are equal or superior to the Americans in space and missile technology.

1959—On New Year's Day, Fidel Castro and his followers take over Cuba; at first, he is welcomed by American leaders.

1960—On May 1, an American U-2 spy plane is shot down over Russian territory triggering heightened Cold War tension between the two countries.

1961—On April 17, anti-Castro Cuban exiles invade
Cuban shores at the Bay of Pigs; the operation
is supported by the United States and it fails,
resulting in the death or capture of the exiles.
In December, Fidel Castro announces he is a
Communist and that he is building a Communist
state in Cuba.

1962—In July, Fidel Castro's brother Raúl, visits the
Soviet Union where the Russian leader, Nikita
Khrushchev, secretly offers to put missiles on
Cuban soil in order to prevent another U.S.
invasion; the Castro government accepts the offer.

October 14: An American U-2 spy plane
photographs fields being cleared by workers;
experts conclude the fields will house missile
launchers.

October 16: A group of Kennedy advisers, a
team that will soon be called ExComm, meet
to discuss what can be done about the Soviet
missiles being put up in Cuba.

October 17: With President Kennedy in
Connecticut, the ExComm men ponder two
possible moves against the missiles: a naval
blockade or an air strike; both could lead to
nuclear war with the USSR.

October 18: Members of ExComm are
dividing into "hawks," who favor aggressive
action, and "doves," who wish to negotiate with
the Soviets; Air Force general Curtis E. LeMay
is the most vocal hawk, and UN ambassador
Adlai Stevenson is the leading dove.

October 19: President Kennedy flies to Ohio
and later to Illinois; he hopes to keep the missile
crisis secret and carry on his regular schedule;
ExComm recommends a naval blockade of Cuba.

October 20: The president is in Chicago when it is announced he has a cold and will have to return to Washington to recover; newspaper writers suspect there is a crisis somewhere in the world.

October 21: U.S. armed forces are put on high alert.

October 22: The president makes a speech to the nation announcing the blockade, which he calls a "quarantine;" in strong language, he urges Khrushchev to withdraw the missiles from Cuba.

October 23: Cuba is surrounded by U.S. naval ships; fear grips the United States; many families flee the cities because they believe urban areas will be targets for A-bombs.

October 24: Most—but not all—Russian ships stop before they reach the American blockade line.

October 25: The first intercept takes place between Soviet and American vessels, there are no incidents; in the United Nations, Ambassador Adlai Stevenson and Soviet delegate Valerian Zorin have a heated exchange.

October 26: Newsman John Scali gets a telephone call from Soviet operative Aleksandr Fomin who asks if the United States would pledge not to invade Cuba in exchange for a Soviet withdrawal of the missiles; later that day, a letter from Khrushchev poses the same question.

October 27: In a potentially dangerous situation at sea, a U.S destroyer confronts a submarine armed with a nuclear torpedo. U-2 pilot Major Rudolf Anderson is shot down and killed over Cuba; he is the only casualty of the missile crisis. Khrushchev sends a second letter to Kennedy, this time demanding the United States remove its missiles from Turkey; Kennedy responds, ignoring the missile trade-off demand.

October 28: Khrushchev announces he is removing the missiles in exchange for an American pledge not to invade Cuba; in a private agreement, the United States said it will soon take its missiles out of Turkey. The Cuban missile crisis is over.

CHAPTER NOTES

Chapter One. Spy in the Sky

1. Norman Polmar and John D. Gresham, *Defcon-2* (Hoboken, N.J.: John Wiley & Sons, Inc., 2006), p. 88.

2. Harold Evans, *The American Century* (New York: Alfred A. Knopf, 2000), p. 492.

3. Don Munton and David A. Welch, *The Cuban Missile Crisis: A Concise History* (New York: Oxford University Press, 2007), p. 48.

Chapter Two. The Cold War and the Arms Race

1. Harold Evans, *The American Century* (New York: Alfred A. Knopf, 2000), p. 391.

2. Harry G. Summers Jr., *Korean War Almanac* (New York: Facts On File, 1990), p. 75.

Chapter Three. Cuba: A Troubled Neighbor

1. Robert F. Kennedy, *Thirteen Days: A Memoir of the Cuban Missile Crisis* (New York: W. W. Norton & Company, 1971), p. 23.

2. Harold Evans, *The American Century* (New York: Alfred A. Knopf, 2000), p. 63.

3. Tad Szule, *Fidel: A Critical Portrait* (New York: William Morrow and Company, Inc., 1986), p. 99.

4. Ibid., p. 100.

5. Don Munton and David A. Welch, *The Cuban Missile Crisis: A Concise History* (New York: Oxford University Press, 2007), p. 12.

6. Aleksandr Fursenko and Timothy Naftali, *"One Hell of a Gamble": The Secret History of the Cuban Missile Crisis, 1958–1964* (New York: W. W. Norton & Co., 1997), p. 9.

7. Ibid., p. 8.

8. Munton and Welch, p. 17.

9. Ibid.

10. Ernest R. May and Philip D. Zelikow, eds., *The Kennedy Tapes: Inside the White House During the Cuban Missile Crisis* (Cambridge: Belknap Press, 1997), p. 25.

11. Ibid., p. 26.

12. Norman Polmar and John D. Gresham, *Defcon-2* (Hoboken, N.J.: John Wiley & Sons, Inc., 2006), p. 6.

Chapter Four. The Crisis Begins

1. Aleksandr Fursenko and Timothy Naftali, *"One Hell of a Gamble": The Secret History of the Cuban Missile Crisis, 1958–1964* (New York: W. W. Norton & Co., 1997), p. 182.

2. Robert F. Kennedy, *Thirteen Days: A Memoir of the Cuban Missile Crisis* (New York: W. W. Norton & Company, 1971), p. 19.

3. Ibid., p. 20.

4. Norman Polmar and John D. Gresham, *Defcon-2* (Hoboken, N.J.: John Wiley & Sons, Inc., 2006), p. 16.

5. Kennedy, p. 25.

6. Ernest R. May and Philip D. Zelikow, eds., *The Kennedy Tapes: Inside the White House During the Cuban Missile Crisis* (Cambridge: Belknap Press, 1997), p. ix.

7. Ibid., p. 63.

8. Kennedy, p. 28.

9. Nikita Khrushchev, trans., Strobe Talbott, *Nikita Khrushchev Remembers* (Boston: Little Brown & Co., 1970), p. 493.

10. Richard Reeves, *President Kennedy: Profile of Power* (New York: Simon and Schuster, 1993), p. 379.

11. Ibid.

12. Ibid., p. 383.

13. Sheldon M. Stern, *The Week the World Stood Still: Inside the Secret Cuban Missile Crisis* (Stanford, Calif.: Stanford University Press, 2005), p. 69.

14. Kennedy, p. 35.

Chapter Five. The Brink of War

1. Richard Reeves, *President Kennedy: Profile of Power* (New York: Simon and Schuster, 1993), p. 386.

2. Norman Polmar and John D. Gresham, *Defcon-2* (Hoboken, N.J.: John Wiley & Sons, Inc., 2006), p. 121.

3. Robert F. Kennedy, *Thirteen Days: A Memoir of the Cuban Missile Crisis* (New York: W. W. Norton & Company, 1971), p. 38.

4. Ibid., p. 41.

5. Reeves, p. 391.

6. Aleksandr Fursenko and Timothy Naftali, *"One Hell of a Gamble": The Secret History of the Cuban Missile Crisis, 1958–1964* (New York: W. W. Norton & Co., 1997), p. 238.

7. Ibid.

8. Reeves, p. 392.

9. Ibid., p. 394.

10. Ibid.

11. "JFK IN HISTORY: Cuban Missile Crisis—Radio and Television Report to the American People on the Soviet Arms Buildup in Cuba, October 22, 1962," *John F. Kennedy Presidential Library and Museum*, n.d., <http://www.jfklibrary.org/Historical+Resources/JFK+in+History/Cuban+Missile+Crisis.htm> (February 5, 2008).

Chapter Six. Enforcing the Quarantine

1. Richard Reeves, *President Kennedy: Profile of Power* (New York: Simon and Schuster, 1993), p. 395.

2. Ibid., p. 397.

3. Norman Polmar and John D. Gresham, *Defcon-2* (Hoboken, N.J.: John Wiley & Sons, Inc., 2006), p. 139.

4. Ibid., p. 135.

5. Reeves, p. 397.

6. Aleksandr Fursenko and Timothy Naftali, *"One Hell of a Gamble:" The Secret History of the Cuban Missile Crisis, 1958–1964* (New York: W. W. Norton & Co., 1997), p. 256.

7. Robert F. Kennedy, *Thirteen Days: A Memoir of the Cuban Missile Crisis* (New York: W. W. Norton & Company, 1971), pp. 52–53.

8. Ibid., p. 54.

9. Ibid., pp. 53–54.

10. Ibid., p. 55.

11. Ibid.

12. Sheldon M. Stern, *The Week the World Stood Still: Inside the Secret Cuban Missile Crisis* (Stanford, Calif.: Stanford University Press, 2005), p. 112

Chapter Seven. Diplomacy at Work

1. Sheldon M. Stern, *The Week the World Stood Still: Inside the Secret Cuban Missile Crisis* (Stanford, Calif.: Stanford University Press, 2005), p. 114.

2. Norman Polmar and John D. Gresham, *Defcon-2* (Hoboken, N.J.: John Wiley & Sons, Inc., 2006), p. 1.

3. Ibid., p. 151.

4. Alice George, *Awaiting Armageddon: How Americans*

Faced the Cuban Missile Crisis (Chapel Hill, N.C.: The University of North Carolina Press, 2003), p. xviii.

5. Richard Reeves, *President Kennedy: Profile of Power* (New York: Simon and Schuster, 1993), pp. 405?406.

6. Ibid., p. 406.

7. Polmar and Gresham, p. 148.

8. George, p. 97.

9. Ibid., p. 94.

10. Polmar and Gresham, p. 186.

11. Ibid.

12. Don Munton and David A. Welch, *The Cuban Missile Crisis: A Concise History* (New York: Oxford University Press, 2007), p. 73.

13. Robert F. Kennedy, *Thirteen Days: A Memoir of the Cuban Missile Crisis* (New York: W. W. Norton & Company, 1971), p. 68.

14. Ibid., p. 69.

15. George, p. xx.

Chapter Eight. Peace at Last

1. Richard Reeves, *President Kennedy: Profile of Power* (New York: Simon and Schuster, 1993), p. 411.

2. Norman Polmar and John D. Gresham, *Defcon-2* (Hoboken, N.J.: John Wiley & Sons, Inc., 2006), p. 162.

3. Ibid.

4. Ibid.

5. Ibid., p. 163.

6. Robert F. Kennedy, *Thirteen Days: A Memoir of the Cuban Missile Crisis* (New York: W. W. Norton & Company, 1971), pp. 73–74.

7. Ibid., p. 70.

8. Ibid., p. 73.

9. Ibid., p. 71.

10. Ibid., p. 77.

11. Sheldon M. Stern, *The Week the World Stood Still: Inside the Secret Cuban Missile Crisis* (Stanford, Calif.: Stanford University Press, 2005), p. 186.

12. Alice George, *Awaiting Armageddon: How Americans Faced the Cuban Missile Crisis* (Chapel Hill, N.C.: The University of North Carolina Press, 2003), p. xxiii.

13. Ibid., p. xxi.

14. Polmar and Gresham, p. 221.

15. Ernest R. May and Philip D. Zelikow. eds., *The Kennedy Tapes: Inside the White House During the Cuban Missile Crisis* (Cambridge: Belknap Press, 1997), pp. 630–631.

16. Kennedy, p. 83.

17. Reeves, p. 424.

Chapter Nine. Reflecting on the Crisis

1. Richard Reeves, *President Kennedy: Profile of Power* (New York: Simon and Schuster, 1993), p. 411.

2. Nikita Khrushchev, trans., Strobe Talbott, *Nikita Khrushchev Remembers* (Boston: Little Brown & Co., 1970), p. 496.

3. Don Munton and David A. Welch, *The Cuban Missile Crisis: A Concise History* (New York: Oxford University Press, 2007), p. 82.

4. Khrushchev, p. 504.

5. Sheldon M. Stern, *The Week the World Stood Still: Inside the Secret Cuban Missile Crisis* (Stanford, Calif.: Stanford University Press, 2005), pp. 195–196.

6. Ibid., p. 196.

7. Norman Polmar and John D. Gresham, *Defcon-2* (Hoboken, N.J.: John Wiley & Sons, Inc., 2006), p. 277.

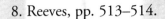

8. Reeves, pp. 513–514.

9. Ibid., p. 514.

10. Polmar and Gresham, p. 284.

11. Munton and Welch, p. 51.

12. Ibid., p. 37.

13. Polmar and Gresham, p. 227.

GLOSSARY

ballistic missile—A missile that is guided up into the atmosphere in a high arch, then free falls toward its target.

catastrophic—Disastrous, terrible.

Cold War—A period from about 1945 to 1991 when the United States and the Soviet Union were locked in conflict, though the two nations never directly engaged in battle with one another.

covert—Hidden or secret.

dilemma—A choice between difficult alternatives.

fraught—Harboring an unseen property, as in, "The mission was fraught with danger."

freeze—In Cold War terms, a time of heightened tension between the capitalist and Communist worlds.

obsolete—Dated to the point of uselessness.

Oval Office—White House office of the president of the United States.

quarantine—To isolate sick people so their disease will not spread; in the Cuban missile crisis, the word was used for *blockade* because it sounded less harsh.

refuge—A hiding place.

scenario—A summary or outline of an action.

sieve—Normally a kitchen-straining device; in political terms the word has been used to describe someone who habitually "leaks" information.

thaw—Cold War language used to describe a period of relaxation and peace between the superpowers.

FURTHER READING

Books on the Cuban Missile Crisis

Byrne, Paul J. *The Cuban Missile Crisis: To the Brink of War*. Mankato, Minn.: Compass Point Books, 2006.

McConnell, William S., ed. *Living Through the Cuban Missile Crisis*. Farmington Hills, Minn.: Greenhaven Press, 2005.

Whiting, Jim. *The Cuban Missile Crisis: The Cold War Goes Hot*. Hockessin, Del.: Mitchel Lane, 2006.

Books on the Cold War

Burgan, Michael. *The Berlin Airlift*. Minneapolis, Minn.: Compass Point Books, 2007.

Gottfried, Ted. *The Cold War*. Brookfield, Conn.: Twenty-First Century Books, 2003.

Hillstrom, Kevin. *The Cold War*. Detroit: Omnigraphics, 2006.

Biographies

Aronson, Marc. *Up Close: Robert F. Kenney: A Twentieth-Century Life*. New York: Viking, 2007.

Butts, Ellen R., and Joyce R. Schwartz. *Fidel Castro*. Minneapolis, Minn.: Lerner Publications Co., 2005.

Miller, Calvin Craig. *Che Guevara: In Search of Revolution*. Greensboro, N.C.: Morgan Reynolds Pub., 2006.

Naden, Corinne J., and Rose Blue. *Fidel Castro and the Cuban Revolution.* Greensboro, N.C.: Morgan Reynolds, 2006.

Sommer, Shelley. *John Kennedy: His Life and Legacy.* New York: HarperCollins, 2005.

Other Books

Coleman, Janet Wyman. *Secrets, Lies, Gizmos, and Spies: A History of Spies and Espionage.* New York: Harry N. Abrams, 2006.

Davis, Mary Byrd, and Arthur H. Purcell. *Weapons of Mass Destruction.* New York: Facts on File, 2006.

Sheehan, Sean, and Leslie Jermyn. *Cuba.* New York: Marshall Cavendish Benchmark, 2005.

Stoff, Laurie. *The Rise and Fall of the Soviet Union.* Farmington Hills, Mich.: Greenhaven Press, 2006.

INTERNET ADDRESSES

Cold War: Cuban Missile Crisis
<http://www.loc.gov/exhibits/archives/colc.html>

The Cuban Missile Crisis
<www.hpol.org/jfk/cuban/>

Contains audio recordings made in Kennedy's office as his team debated the U.S. response to the Russian missiles.

Days in October: The Cuban Missile Crisis
<http://library.thinkquest.org/11046/>

INDEX